Following Jesus
The Nature of Christian Discipleship

Following Jesus

The Nature of Christian Discipleship

James E. Carter

Broadman Press
Nashville, Tennessee

4282-53
ISBN: 0-8054-8253-9

Dewey Decimal Classification: 248.6
Subject headings: CHRISTIAN LIFE // DISCIPLESHIP
Library of Congress Catalog Card Number: 77-073439
Printed in the United States of America

Dedicated to
J. H. and Louise Templin Hunter
My Parents-in-Law

Preface

Discipleship is no optional matter for the Christian. If you are a Christian you *are* a disciple.

As Christians we do not have a choice about whether we will be disciples. We become disciples of Jesus Christ when we accept him as personal Savior. The only choice we have is to the kind of discipleship we will display, whether we will be good disciples or bad, or a mixture of the two.

The New Testament is big on discipleship. The word *decision* does not occur one time in the New Testament. We hear and use that word quite a bit in *our* religious talk. Even though the concept is there, the word is never found in the New Testament. The word *disciple*, though, in both its noun and verb forms shows up numerous times in the New Testament.

We are to be disciples and we are to make disciples. That becomes quite clear in reading the New Testament.

Basically, discipleship is following Jesus. This means *following* Jesus not *following after* Jesus. It involves patterning our lives after him, learning from him, identifying with him, and living for him.

There are many facets of discipleship. In this book I do not pretend to have covered every facet of discipleship. I do intend to have presented an overview of what it means to follow Jesus and how this is applied in several areas of our lives. While it may not go from Dan to Beersheba, it does go from the acceptance of Christ and discipleship to the possibility of defection from discipleship and to the living out of our discipleship in these decisive days.

Through preaching, teaching, and discussing, this material has been shared and shaped in one form or another with the people of the First Baptist Church, Natchitoches, Louisiana, which I served as pastor for thirteen years, as well as with other churches and groups with which I have shared life and ministry through the years.

The typescript was prepared by Mrs. Carolyn Lee who served with me as secretary for many years in her usual amiable and efficient way. I am appreciative of her help and friendship. I am also appreciative of the church and its people who have helped to shape these ideas even though they do not have to take the responsibility for them. And for my family, who is willing to share me and my time with books and a typewriter, I am always grateful.

Through this book I trust that we will all come to know and to appreciate a little more the nature of Christian discipleship, as it is expressed through following Jesus.

Contents

1

The Call to Discipleship

Beethoven's Fifth Symphony in C Minor is built around a single phrase of music. It has four notes: one short note repeated three times, followed immediately by a longer note lower down the scale. This phrase is repeated throughout the symphony. It gives a rugged rhythm and momentum. It also gives it a memorable quality. You can whistle that symphony.

If you are a devotee of television, you would recognize the notes from the Vanquish commercial. You know, the question that is an assertion, "Have I got something for your headache?" Then comes the *V* for victory sign, and these stirring notes.

If you went to the silent movies, you would recognize them as the theme when the burglar came into the house or the villain rounded the corner.

If you are a historian, you would know that during World War II it was this musical phrase which became the secret *V* sign, the victory sign, for conquered Europe.

Does this haunting four-note sequence have any particular meaning? Apparently so. Tradition has it that Beethoven himself said that it represents, "Thus fate knocks at the door." [1] Whether that is true, it is certain that these dramatic opening notes, repeated and reechoed all the way through, do convey, with extraordinary vividness, a rap, a summons to draw back the bolt, open the door, answer the summons, to stand.

But is it fate that knocks at the door? Christians feel it is Christ.

It was at another time that men were engaged in their daily occupations when they received a call from Christ. Jesus Christ knocked at their doors. Because the time is different or because the circumstances were different does not make either of the experiences any less Christ's call. The story is told in Mark 1:16-20.

Jesus, this time, was walking along the shores of the Sea of Galilee, when he chanced upon Andrew and Simon, later to be known as Simon Peter, casting their nets into the sea. These were probably the round hand nets used for catching a few fish. He immediately stopped and said to them, "Come ye after me, and I will make you to become fishers of men" (v. 17). This was Christ's call to discipleship to them. He went a little farther down the shore. This time he saw James and John working over their nets in the boat with their father and the other men who worked with them. Though the exact words are not given, we can imagine that he said something similar to them, "Come ye after me." And they received Christ's call to discipleship.

Probably these men knew Christ already. Even though Mark presents this as the first preaching of Christ in Galilee, John indicates that he had preached previously in Judea. John tells us of Andrew's introduction to Jesus and his going to bring his brother Simon to Christ. So, these men knew him. They may have even gone with him before as he preached in Judea. But now they were home again. They were about their usual business of fishing. Things had lapsed into the regular routine of life. But all of this was interrupted with Christ's call: "Come ye after me." Life could never be the same again. They had heard Christ's call and they had responded.

Does Christ still call us to come and follow him? He surely does. Whether by the seashore of Galilee, or relaxed at home, or mending nets in the boat with the father, or sitting in a pew in church, Christ offers his call to people. It is a call to come after him. The call to accept Christ is a call to discipleship.

Command

Jesus said to them, "Come ye after me." These men had known Jesus before. They had heard him preach. Possibly they had traveled with him. But now he came to them with a command. Everything about this command centers around a personal relationship.

It is a command to a person. He said, "Come *ye* . . . ." This is addressed personally to those approached by Jesus. There can be no escaping this. There can be no doubt to whom it is offered. It is directed personally to the individual.

And this is the way Christ approaches us. The call to accept Christ as Savior and to come after him as disciples is personally directed to each of us. It is impossible to accept Christ by proxy, or for someone else to do it for you. Jesus confronts each of us individually. It is our decision and we must make it. So is the call to service after having met Christ. This, too, is personally directed. Christ approaches each of us and challenges us with the best that we can do for him. And we must each, personally, make the decision whether we will be nominal, useless Christians, or whether we will be useful, working servants of God. Martin Luther once said, "Let no man lose the faith that God willeth to do a great work through him."

Adoniram Judson is remembered and revered for his place in the foreign mission enterprise. By his adoption of Baptist views while en route to India, then to Burma, he propelled American Baptists into foreign missions. He came to a personal decision about his involvement in foreign missions while a student at Andover Theological Seminary in Massachusetts. For some time he had brooded about foreign missions in general, and Burma in particular. On a cold February day in 1910, Judson made his decision. He testified, "It was during a solitary walk in the woods behind the college, while meditating and praying on the subject, and feeling half inclined to give it up, that the command of Christ, 'Go into all the world and preach the Gospel to every creature,' was presented to my mind with such clearness and power that I came to a full decision, and though great difficulties appeared in my way, resolved to obey the command at all events." [2] Judson obeyed a command to a person.

And it is a command about a person. Notice that Jesus commanded, "Come ye after *me*."

This is basic to Christianity. We are Christians because we follow Christ. He does not come to offer us a theological system, or an ethical system, or a nice way of life. He offers us a personal relationship to himself. That is the way it was for the early disciples, and that is the way it must be for us.

It was very early in the Christian experience that one of these same persons who answered the command of Jesus said to others, "Neither is there salvation in any other: for there is none other name under heaven given among men, whereby we must be saved" (Acts 4:12). And this but echoes the words of the Savior himself who said, "And I, if I be lifted up from the earth, will draw all men unto me" (John 12:32).

A disciple is one who follows another. The personal nature of Christianity demands that it turn on a personal relationship with Jesus Christ as Savior. It is Christ who is followed.

Commission

Christ's call is also a commission. To those first followers Jesus said, "I will make you to become fishers of men."

This commission is a task. Here is a job that is offered to these people. It is not as though they had no job. When he found them, they were busy at their occupation. Perhaps the very thing that they were doing suggested the metaphor which Jesus used. They had been fishers of fish; from henceforth they would be fishers of men.

This is a task that is incumbent upon every Christian. Whatever our regular task, this also becomes our task. To be farmers of men, to be builders of men, to be salesmen to men, to be accountants of men—whatever we regularly do—this also we must do if we have met Christ and experienced his grace, if we have heard his call.

Someone has said that what every man needs is "something in

which he can invest his life." So Jesus did not call his men to a comfortable ease or to a passive and a lethargic inactivity; he called them to a task in which they would have to give themselves. He called them to a task in which they could only win something for themselves by giving their all to him and to others. Lyman Beecher was once asked what was the greatest thing that a human being could do. His reply was to bring another to Jesus Christ as Savior. This we often call today a lay ministry. It is the understanding that all Christians have a ministry. All of us are commissioned by Christ to the task of witnessing for him.

And this is a promise. Jesus gives no call without a promise. Observe some of the calls and accompanying promises he has given to us. The call is "come unto me, all ye that labour and are heavy laden." With that call is the promise, "and I will give you rest" (Matt. 12:28). "Behold, I stand at the door and knock." But he also promises, "If any man hear my voice, and open the door, I will come in to him, and will sup with him, and he with me" (Rev. 3:20). To these men he called, "Come ye after me" and he promised, "and I will make you to become fishers of men."

Whenever Christ gives us a call, he also gives us a promise that we will have the strength sufficient for that call and to do that task.

C. Roy Angell recorded in *God's Gold Mines,* an incident from the life of Dr. James Parrish, who once served as vice-president of Stetson University. Here it is in his own words.

Dr. James Parrish, vice-president of Stetson University, and one of the great preachers of the South, made this message live for all his audience when he spoke at the Florida Baptist Convention in Pensacola.

"I came from the country" he said, "and had never had the privilege of hearing any great preachers. So, when I finally got down to Stetson and found that Roland Leavell was coming to the campus for a revival, I was all agog with excitement and anticipation. The first night of the revival I was on the front seat, smiling and happy. Dr. Leavell was at his best, and the sermon was a masterpiece. But long before it was over, the smile had left my face.

After the service, I went back to my room. I was miserable. The thought kept ringing through my mind, God doesn't need me. I could never preach like that. Maybe I have made a mistake, and God hasn't even called me to the ministry.'' It was a long, miserable night.

The next evening, I sat about midway, and once more there was no joy in my heart. The sermon was wonderful, and I was convinced more than ever that God just couldn't use me.

The third night I was on the back seat, downhearted, as I listened to another powerful message. When it was over, I went out and lay down on my face in the campus grass and wept. I was ready to give up and go home, and then God seemed to speak to me. He quoted his own words from the first Psalm, "He . . . bringeth forth his fruit in his season.''

I lay there for a long time and finally said, "Well, Lord, if you can use me, you can have all of me. I will use my little one talent to preach in some small country church and do my best for thee." [3]

This commission involves a process. Jesus made that clear when he said, "I will make you to *become* fishers of men."

We often overlook this when reading this verse of Scripture. Christ has called each of us to service. He has promised each of us a task and victory in that task. But he also tells us that it will have to be a process of growth. He indicates that it will take a while before we are developed, efficient fishers of men.

We are usually not willing for this process to develop. We become so impatient. People who buy instant mashed potatoes, TV dinners, and brown-and-serve rolls are not much given to patience. We are unwilling to let anything develop. We want results and we want those results instantly. But it takes a time of walking with Christ, of following him, of seeking his will, and of studying his Word to really become the disciples we should be. We become disciples when we accept his call. A commission is inherent in the call. But we must constantly and continuously develop to become full-grown disciples.

Committal

Christ's call demands committal. I can never read this incident without paying attention to that word *straightway* as it is used here. It is one of Mark's favorite words. It tells something of the realistic vividness that Mark puts in the gospel message. We would probably translate it today "immediately." But to me it gives a vivid picture of response to Christ. He came to them and said, "Come after me," and immediately they complied with his request; they responded to his call.

This is some of the readiness that we need in following Christ. Too often we are like the man who bought the field, or the man who married a wife, or the man who wanted to wait until his father died. We are willing to work for Christ, to serve him, but we want to wait a little longer to do it. How refreshing this is! And how pleasing it must be to Christ.

In this same spirit I can think of the persecutor Saul down on his knees on the Damascus road as he cries out, "What wilt thou have me do?" Or I can think of the boy Samuel, as the wise old Eli let him know that it was God who called in the night. He said for Samuel to answer, "Speak, Lord; for thy servant heareth" (1 Sam. 3:9). I can think of Amos who answered the high priest Amaziah when he was told to prophesy in Judah, but not in Israel. Amos said, "I was no prophet, neither was I a prophet's son; but I was an herdsman and a gatherer of sycamore fruit: And the Lord took me as I followed the flock and said unto me, Go, prophesy unto my people Israel" (Amos 7:14-15). And there he was in Israel, prophesing away. This is something of the spirit of Andrew and Simon, and James and John. It is a spirit of readiness to respond to God's call. This same spirit of readiness ought to characterize us. If it did, we would see a more ready response to the opportunities to minister in Christ's name, a greater sensitivity to human needs, and a willingness to witness.

In this is seen also an urgency. To straightway leave what you are doing to follow Christ is to sense something of the urgency of this matter of Christian service. Perhaps we are no more urgent because we are no more concerned. It really does not seem to matter that people all around us need to hear the gospel and need to be confronted with the claims of Christ. If we had something of this spirit of urgency about us, then we would have more of a sense of loyalty to Christ and the church. Church and Christ's cause would come to mean more to us than the school, the lodge, the civic club, the bridge club, or the Little League. The cause of Christ becomes unimportant to us when we lose the sense of urgency.

From this matter of committal we see something of what it means to commit oneself to Christ. It means abandonment. They left their nets. They left their boats. They left their father. When Christ confronted them with his call, everything else became secondary. This became a costly decision for them. They left all that they had, which is the minimum requirement for Christians.

Dietrich Bonhoeffer said that when Christ calls a man he bids him come and die. If necessary, all must be abandoned in order that we can stand before Christ ready to serve and ready to do his bidding. There are some things that are surely fine. They are good amusement. They provide good family entertainment. But when these things come to take the place of Christ and Christian service and loyalty to Christ's church, then they stand in the way of Christ and his cause. They actually become enemies of Christ. The things are not enemies; they are entirely neutral. It is how we use them that makes them enemies. There are a lot of people who, because of this, are going to have to answer to God for their boats—and their golf—and their television—and their cards—and their fishing—and their hunting—and their coffee—and their weekend trips.

This is it! The matter of committing yourself to Christ. Have you heard his call? In your own mind and heart have you heard his command, "Come," and his commission, "I will make you to become fishers of men," but have not been willing to make the committal of your life to him? In John Bunyan's dream, Christian came in his journeying with Interpreter to the Palace which was heavily guarded and into which it was a battle to seek an entry. At the door there sat the man with the inkhorn taking the names of those who would dare the assault. All were hanging back; then Christian saw "a man of a very stout countenance come up to the man that sat there to write saying, 'Set down my name, sir.' " Can you really say that to Christ, knowing that he will want you to live the maximum

Christian life, knowing that he will want you to be a witness to him?

This is Christ's call. You cannot really escape it. You might run and hide and delude yourself. But wherever you are the call comes ringing after you. "Come ye after me," he keeps on saying to us.

Whenever Christ calls a person to himself, he calls him to salvation and discipleship. The two go together. Discipleship is not an optional matter to be decided later. It is the very heart of the personal nature of salvation. Christ calls you to himself.

2

A Definition of Discipleship

The word *disciple* is really not just a religious word. A disciple is a learner. The English word that translates the New Testament word for disciple shows that. A disciple is one who follows another and learns from him.

We have taken the word *disciple* and have given it a specialized religious meaning. But it is not simply and solely a religious word. We use it in popular speech to indicate that one has followed another's leadership, scholarship, or style.

For instance, if I were a football coach (and if you could see me you would know immediately that this is a supposition purely for illustration), and it were said that I was a disciple of the late Vince Lombardi, what would it mean? Well, it would not mean that I look like Vince Lombardi. Even though kink for kink I could probably match his curly hair and inch for inch I could match the space between his two front teeth, it would not mean that I look like the late Vince Lombardi. It would mean that I would do the things that he did. It would mean that I was good at those things that distinguished him. For a football coach to be a disciple of Vince Lombardi it would mean that he majored on conditioning and the fundamentals of football.

Now let me hazard a definition of discipleship. For years, I tried to find a good working definition of discipleship. While I do not claim originality for this definition, I think it might help in the understanding of discipleship.[1] And in presenting it I am aware that I will offend every English teacher I ever had, or of whom I have ever heard. Here it is: *a disciple of Jesus Christ is one who follows Jesus and is good at the things that Jesus was good at.*

If you are a disciple of Jesus Christ and follow him, then it will mean that you do the things that he did, that you are good at the things at which Jesus was good.

We get some help from Jesus' discourse to his first disciples in John 15. There Jesus gave them the analogy of the vine and the branches. He was as a vine; they were as branches. Branches seek to reproduce the life and the activity of the vine. They will do the same things that the vine does.

Jesus gave emphasis in this passage to the fruit that the branches would bear. And they could not bear the same kind of fruit he did unless they were good at the same things he was. The fruit of a Christian is a Christlike life.

Jesus was talking to these early disciples, these learners, shortly before his death. He was trying to prepare them for his death. But more than that, he was trying to prepare them for their life. He was trying to prepare them for life without him. This is how they were to live. This is how they were to act. These were the things they were to expect. This was the strength they could have. This was what they were to be.

What are you good at? Whom do you follow in life? To be a disciple of Jesus Christ means following Jesus and being good at the things that he was good at.

Life

If you are a disciple of Jesus Christ, it will show in your life. You will be good at living.

Someone once said that Christians who are children of the living God ought to major in living. When Jesus gave the analogy of the vine and the branches, he was talking about living, not about dying. The vine is a living thing; the branches live because the vine lives.

But it is also apparent that the sustenance of our lives as Christians is from Christ. The branches can only live as they draw sustenance and strength from the vine. We can only live as we draw sustenance and strength from Christ.

Initially, we come to new life through faith in Jesus Christ. He is the source of life for us. As we recognize our need, confess our sin, and accept him through faith we are introduced to that abundant life of which he spoke.

Life is also sustained through Christ. The Christian life is a life of faith in God through Christ from beginning to end. It is initiated by faith; it is sustained by faith.

One of the marks of this life that we have in Christ is joy. Notice that in John 15:11 Jesus said, "These things I have spoken to you, that my joy may be in you, and that your joy may be full" (RSV).[2] We have joy in life as we gain joy through Christ. Our lives are dependent upon him. Our lives must be lived as his.

There is a distinctiveness about Christian joy. Just as there is a difference in Christ's peace and the world's peace so is there a difference in Christ's joy and the world's joy. In John 14:27 Jesus had said, "Peace I leave with you; my peace I give to you; not as the world gives do I give to you" (RSV).

The world's kind of peace is negative; peace is considered the absence of strife. Jesus' kind of peace is positive; it is a peace even in the midst of strife.

And so it is with the joy that the Christian has through Christ. It is a joy that can sing in spite of circumstances.

The late Sam Shoemaker once identified joy as the "surest mark of a Christian."[3] Of all the other things that could be used to identify the Christian—faith, love, hope—joy stands as the surest mark.

Shoemaker quoted Paul Tillich who remarked, "Is our lack of joy due to the fact that we are Christians, or to the fact that we are not sufficiently Christian?"[4]

And that may be getting close to the mark. We have not experienced the true joy of knowing Christ because we have not been willing to know Christ completely. As Christ comes into our lives and we follow him then we will become good at living. This life we live in discipleship will have joy as one of its distinguishing marks. Jesus talked about his joy in the very shadow of the cross. And we can live with joy in the shadow of those depressing situations that may threaten us.

Love

Also, as a disciple of Jesus Christ you will be good at loving. The Christian life is a life of love.

Christians are sent out into the world to love one another. In fact, Jesus gave love as a characteristic mark of discipleship. In John 13:35 he said, "By this all men will know that you are my disciples, if you have love for one another" (RSV).

There are times when Christians act as though they were to argue with, antagonize, or to outdo one another. But Jesus indicated that we are to love one another.

Love issues in mercy and compassion. When love is present mercy and compassion will also be present.

Theodore F. Adams is credited with the story of the last planeload of Dutch colonists who left Indonesia when it became an independent nation.

Among those who were waiting in the airport for the plane that would take them home to the Netherlands as the nation became free were a general and a poet. Many of those people had spent their lives in Indonesia while it was a Dutch colony. While they were Dutch, they would not be at home in Holland; home was Indonesia.

The general was pacing up and down in the airport. As he paced he was questioning out loud. He was asking why the people hated them so. They had brought Western civilization to them; they had built roads, cities, and schools. Why should there be such hate toward them?

Then the poet answered. He replied that perhaps the reason they hated them was the look that was in their eyes when the Dutch people spoke to them.

True love is not measured by particular acts when these acts are performed out of self-interest rather than love. When there is love, it will show in mercy and compassion toward other people.

This love, mercy, and compassion will show. The old song proclaimed that love and marriage go together like a horse and a carriage. Since that is true, love and mercy will show in the loving acts that are performed.

Indeed it does take a lot of love to make a pound. When you measure the amount of love that it takes to bring a child from infancy to maturity, it takes a lot of loving. When you measure the amount of love it takes to bring a Christian from a babe in Christ to a mature, witnessing, ministering Christian, it takes a lot of loving.

That love can be expressed in many ways. It may be the love that accepts that person for what he is, even when he is unlovely and unloving, and seeks to bring him into conformity to the character of Christ. It may be the love that is willing to stay longer than is demanded in order to see that another person receives proper care in his personal crisis. It may be the love that does what is needed, not what is expected. Anyone can do what is expected. It takes Christian love to do more than is expected; to do what is needed.

Jesus showed us how. It is not an uncharted course that we are to follow. Jesus expressed it himself in John 15:13 when he said, "Greater love has no man than this, that a man lay down his life for his friends" (RSV).

If Jesus defined that greater love as the love that would go even to the point of self-sacrifice, he demonstrated it, too. When Jesus voluntarily laid down his life for us, he gave us the greatest demonstration of love that the world has ever seen. It would be impossible to duplicate this kind of love. It is possible to emulate it. We are to be as loving to one another as Jesus is to us.

But our immediate reaction is that they may be self-defeating. If we show that kind of love, we may not get all that is coming to us. We may allow someone else to get ahead of us. And we may allow our own interest to be overshadowed by someone else's good.

And that is just the point. We have been taught to "look out for number one." And in looking out for ourselves we may become so self-assertive and self-serving that we forget to be loving. Jesus expects those who follow him to be loving. Had he taken his own self-interest to heart he would never have gone to the cross. And had he never gone to the cross we would never have salvation. This is truly the greater love that will willingly give oneself for another. One of the ways the world has caused Christians to conform to its norm is in looking so much toward self-interest. One of the ways Jesus has of transforming us into his kind of disciples is in giving ourselves in love to him and to others.

Hope

Another thing that shows up in Christian discipleship is hope. If you are a disciple of Jesus Christ, you will be good at hoping. The Christian disciple's life is a life of hope.

Did you catch the note of victory in reading John 15? Remember, Jesus was making last minute preparations for a death that he knew was imminent. What he said at that time could have been dismal. It could have been depressive. It could have been sorrowful. But it was not. It was victorious.

Jesus spoke with the scent of victory in the air. He knew that he would die. But he also knew that by his death he would defeat sin, death, and Satan. Thus he could speak with victory and hope.

Where is our hope? We follow that same Jesus. But often we act depressed. Often we act defeated. We act as though sin and death have defeated us, rather than that they have been defeated through Jesus' victory.

God has given us hope. We know what the final outcome will be. While we live in the midst of some depressing circumstances, we know the ultimate outcome. While it seems that death has defeated us, as it is the final foe that we face in life, we know that death is defeated. While it may seem that the power of sin, evil, and wickedness all but engulfs us, we know that the ultimate power of evil over the lives of persons has been broken by Jesus Christ. As Christians we know what the final outcome will be. In the end, God will reign victorious over it all.

The person who reads mystery thrillers will often look to the back of the book to discover the solution before he has worked his way through the book to the solution. The Christian has read the last page of the book of life already. We have hope because of the victory of Christ through the cross and the resurrection.

I once heard Kenneth Chafin, pastor of the South Main Baptist Church in Houston, Texas, tell of an incident from his college experience. While a student at the University of New Mexico, he had to take another English course. And the course that he took was in Shakespeare. It was not necessarily his choice, but it was an English course and it was taught at a time that would fit his schedule. So he took the Shakespeare course.

The professor in that course was enamored with Shakespeare's *Hamlet*. It seemed that he thought that was the most significant thing Shakespeare ever wrote. So they studied *Hamlet* thoroughly. They read it; they discussed it; they analyzed it; and they even memorized part of it.

Then when it seemed that there was nothing else they could do to *Hamlet*, Sir Laurence Olivier's movie "Hamlet" came to the campus theater. And their assignment was to see *Hamlet*.

On the way to the theater to carry out the assignment Chafin ran into a boy he knew at the student center. When the boy asked where he was going and he replied to the movie, the boy wanted to know if he could go with him. He had nothing better to do that afternoon. And Chafin agreed that he could.

Well, this fellow had not been in the Shakespeare course. He had never heard of *Hamlet*. He was just spending an afternoon at the movies. On the way in he bought a bag of popcorn, then settled down to enjoy the film.

But, he got interested in the movie. When things got exciting, he asked Chafin, "What do you think will happen next?" And Chafin told him. Then later he would say, "How will he get out of this?" And Chafin told him. Throughout the movie he would make those kinds of inquiring comments, only to be given the answer.

When the movie was completed and they left the theater, the friend also left Chafin. As he walked away down the sidewalk Chafin shook his head and observed, "Poor guy. Poor guy. He was probably the only person in the house who didn't know the ending."

As Christians who follow Jesus we know the ending. And it gives to us hope.

So you follow Jesus. This means that you are his disciple. This means that you will try to be good at the things that Jesus was good at.

But what about it? How have you done? What are you good at?

I guess what I have been trying to emphasize in this chapter is illustrated by a story that has made the rounds for a long time. But it is illustrative of what it means to follow Jesus.

It seems that there was a little crippled boy who ran a small newsstand in a railroad station. Every day he would sell candy, gum, notions, and newspapers to the people who passed through the station.

One day two men were rushing through the crowded station to catch a train. One of them was ten or fifteen yards in front of the other. Their train was to leave in just a matter of minutes.

The first man turned a corner, ran right into the boy, and knocked him off his stool. Candy, newspapers, gum, and change were scattered everywhere. Without so much as stopping, he spoke harshly to the boy for being there and went on his way.

In just a matter of seconds the other man got to the scene. He gently picked up the boy, made sure that he was all right, and then picked up the scattered newspapers, gum, and change. Then he took out his billfold and gave the boy some money saying, "Here. I think that will take care of any money we did not find or anything that has gotten lost or broken."

Then he picked up his suitcase and hurried on down the track to catch the train that was to depart very shortly. As he hurried down the track, the little crippled boy cupped his hands to his mouth and called, ''Hey, mister! Hey, mister! Are you Jesus Christ?''

To which the man replied, ''No, son. I am just one of his followers who is trying to do what he would do if he were here.'' That is what it means to be a disciple of Jesus Christ.

3

Preparation for Discipleship

General Douglas MacArthur's father, Arthur MacArthur, was also a military officer. Therefore, Douglas MacArthur spent his growing-up years at various military bases. He did not have the opportunity of sustained schooling for his high school education. When he got ready to take the competitive examinations for appointment to West Point, he went to Milwaukee and entered high school. He also established a rigid study schedule to prepare for the exams.

In his autobiography, *Reminiscences,* he said: "When the marks were counted, I led. My careful preparation had repaid me. It was a lesson I never forgot. Preparedness is the key to success and victory." [1]

This is a good lesson for each of us to learn. Preparation is truly a key to success and victory in almost every area of life. We want our teachers to be prepared. We would not consider a physician who had not been adequately prepared and seasoned.

And we seek to prepare ourselves. Schooling is preparation. In making decisions we try to get the background, research the problem, and understand as much about both the alternatives and the outcomes as possible. This is preparation. We prepare for marriage and a family. We prepare for family trips. We prepare for our life's work. We know that nothing happens simply by chance. Preparation is essential in every area of life.

If that is true, why do we spend so little time and effort in preparation for discipleship? Discipleship begins when you accept Jesus Christ as your personal Savior. Discipleship then continues throughout your Christian life.

Discipleship is not one of your options as a Christian. You cannot decide whether you will be a disciple. You can only decide what kind of disciple you will be. In the seventeenth century a man named Thomas Hobson rented horses in Cambridge, England. Hobson had a rule: anyone who rented one of his horses had to take the horse nearest the door. It did not matter what a person's rank, status, or income. It did not matter what his personal choice for a mount might be. If anyone rented a horse from Thomas Hobson he had to take the horse nearest the door. Soon that came to be known as Hobson's Choice. Hobson's Choice is no choice at all. And that is the way it is with Christian discipleship. We have no choice about whether we will be disciples when we become Christians. Our only choice has to do with what kind of disciples we will be—good or bad.

This makes the preparation for discipleship very important.

But what is involved in preparation for discipleship? For some guidance with this question look at some of the very earliest disciples. At the Day of Pentecost Simon Peter preached with great power. There were amazing results: three thousand persons became followers of Jesus Christ.

Some of these persons likely had some previous exposure to Jesus and his teachings. It is logical to assume, though, that a large number of them had no previous experience with Jesus. The book of Acts seems to indicate that many of these people were Jews who had come from around the Mediterranean world for the observance of the Passover and then stayed on for the major feast day of Pentecost. But at Pentecost they got more than they had bargained for; they received Christ too. If they, then, were to follow Christ in discipleship, they would need some preparation for discipleship. In one of those summary statements that turns up from time to time in the book of Acts we are given some indication of this preparation. First we are told that they were made a part of the young church: "Then they that gladly received his word were baptized: and the same day there were added unto them about three thousand souls" (Acts 2:41). But notice what followed this: "And they continued steadfastly in the apostles' doctrine and fellowship, and in breaking of bread, and in prayers" (Acts 2:42).

So obviously a part of their preparation for discipleship involved teaching and training, fellowship, worship, and the opportunities for witness and ministry.

These same elements are present when we prepare for discipleship. If we want to have success and victory, growth and development, mission and ministry, we will need to prepare for discipleship as we prepare for other areas of life.

A Willing Heart

Discipleship begins with a willing heart.

Implicit in the whole matter of discipleship is the acceptance of Jesus Christ as personal Savior. This is the willingness to give ourselves to him in faith and commitment. The heart must be willing before the road of discipleship can be traveled.

When Jesus began to gather the people around him who would form the nucleus of his movement, those people we usually identify as the disciples, he said to them, "Follow me" (Mark 1:17, RSV). And follow they did. They had willing hearts. They were willing to follow Christ.

The name of Keith Miller has become very familiar in the church renewal movement. Miller was willing to share with others his own innermost feelings and experiences with God. This has encouraged others to do so. His first book, *The Taste of New Wine,* not only propelled him onto the religious scene in America but also established some patterns in that type of confessional writing. He had sought to find his own peace with God through many ways including church involvement and seminary attendance.

But let him tell the story of his conversion to Christ.

". . . I felt things closing in on me in the inner chamber of my life.

"I used to walk down the streets, I remember, and suddenly would break out in a cold sweat. I thought I might be losing my mind. One day it was so bad that I got in my company car and took off on a field trip alone. As I was driving through the tall pine woods country of East Texas I suddenly pulled up beside the road and stopped. I remember sitting there in complete despair. I had always been an optimistic person and had always had the feeling that there was one more bounce in the ball. After a good night's sleep one could always start again tomorrow. But now there was no tomorrow in my situation. I was like a man on a great gray treadmill going no place, in a world that was made up of black, black clouds all around me.

"As I sat there I began to weep like a little boy, which I suddenly realized I was inside. I looked up toward the sky. There was nothing I wanted to do with my life. And I said, 'God, if there's anything you want in this stinking soul, take it.'

"That was almost ten years ago. But something came into my life that day which has never left. There wasn't any ringing of bells or flashing of lights or visions: but it was a deep intuitive realization of what it is God wants from a man, which I had never known before. And the peace which came with this understanding was not an experience in itself, but was rather a cessation of the conflict of a lifetime. I realized then that God does not want a man's money, nor does He primarily want his time, even the whole lifetime of it a young seminarian is ready to give Him. God, I realized, doesn't want your time. He wants your *will;* and if you give Him your will, He'll begin to show you life as you've never seen it before.

"It *is* like being born again. I saw that I had not seen Christ at Seminary because I had never known God personally." [2]

The willing heart is where we always begin with God. God does indeed want your will. That is where discipleship begins. And that is where the preparation for discipleship begins.

But this submission of the will to the Lord is not simply a onetime matter. Jesus talked about taking up the cross *daily* to follow him. The willing heart is always willing to follow Christ, to understand more about him, to seek his will.

When you become a disciple of Jesus Christ, you transfer your allegiance. Perhaps your allegiance had been based on yourself, your own desires, your own ambitions, your own self-sufficiency, or your own goals. But with the acceptance of Christ you also transfer your allegiance to him. There is a willingness to die to self and to live for him.

A Willing Head

The preparation for discipleship also involves a willing head. Whenever you become a Christian, you do not park your mind at the door of the church building. We are told to "Love the Lord thy God . . . with thy mind" (Matt. 22:37). And our minds must surely be put to work in loving and serving God.

These earliest disciples "devoted themselves to the apostle's teaching" (Acts 2:42, RSV). They were taught the content of the Christian faith. They were taught the meaning of discipleship with Jesus. They were taught the application of Jesus' teaching.

Growth is a condition of discipleship. If a disciple is a learner, then growth is implied in the very difinition of the word.

The saddest situations of all are those in which growth never occurs. As I write this the cutest, fuzziest, little puppy dog sits at my feet. He is curled up around a shoe, napping. He will wake up and explore the study a bit, bite at my ankle, or untie my shoelace. Then he will snuggle up against a leg, inviting me to reach down and pet him, or pick him up to stroke him. There is scarcely anything in the world as cute as a small puppy. Now he is six weeks old. That is exactly how he should be at six weeks of age. But if by the time he has reached six years of age he is still round, cuddly, and fuzzy, we will know that something is wrong. If by that time he still behaves in the same manner of exploring all the corners, sniffing all the furniture, and untying every shoe lace in sight, we will need to be concerned about him. We expect him to grow. And hopefully he will.

Growth is expected of the disciple of Jesus Christ too. When one has been a Christian for many years and still has not grown or developed beyond those opening stages, we will suspect that something is wrong. And there will be.

There are some means of growth. There are some things that any Christian can do to help himself grow. What it takes is a willing head. The Christian who is willing to use his head and to apply himself can and should grow in grace.

Some of these means of growth may seem a bit elementary. But we never outgrow them. Occasionally we try to go off on some tangent of development, only to realize that we are off beam and are called back to them. Like the compass needle that always swings to the north, we constantly swing back to these same means of Christian growth.

They are mentioned in the experience of those early believers.

Bible study.—We cannot grow as Christians without studying the Bible. We sometimes say that the Bible is the road map to life. If it is going to guide us into life, we will have to read it, study it, and let it guide us. Even the best map cannot guide you if you ignore it.

In the church the Sunday School has the basic responsibility of teaching the Bible. Baptists have set up Sunday School for all ages because we feel very strongly that you never outgrow your need for the study of the Bible.

In addition to Sunday School, however, each person ought to engage in his own study of the Bible. It may be the systematic reading of the Bible through, or the topical study of various topics in the Bible, the mastering of a Bible book at a time, or the following of a simple guide to Bible study and interpretation. Whatever method is used, individual study of the Bible is important for the growing Christian.

Doctrine.—The apostles' teaching also included some doctrine. We are in dire need of a greater doctrinal understanding. It is true that the person who does not stand for something will fall for anything. One basic reason that so many sincere Christians are swept into aberrant beliefs, cults, and movements is that they simply do not have a doctrinal foundation.

In the construction of a new building it always seems that an inordinate amount of time is taken with the foundation. But the foundation is essential. Without a foundation the whole building will crumble. The outside might look very appealing. The interior might be tastefully decorated. But with no foundation there is no lasting building; soon it will all crumble. Because there is little foundation of Christian doctrine many people's commitments also begin to crumble.

Church involvement.—They also continued in the apostles' fellowship. We do not live alone. Someone has said that there is no such thing as solitary religion. We need the fellowship of one another. We need the strength we can derive from one another. We need the witness of one another. Jesus went to the stated worship services customarily. If the Savior himself needed that kind of fellowship with believers, we need it much more.

The "breaking of bread" often had a rather technical meaning referring to the Lord's Supper. At times, though, it had reference to table fellowship. Whichever meaning, or both, is taken it obviously reminds us of the importance of church involvement.

Prayer.—You will notice that prayer was a part of the pattern with these new believers. We never outgrow the need for prayer either. Prayer must be a part of our lives as we express our praise, our needs, and our pleas to God. But prayer is also a part of the listening process as God speaks to us. In this way we have communion with the very Lord of life. Prayer is not simply the last refuge as we turn to God when all else has failed. Prayer should be the daily communion of the believer with the Savior.

One thing remains to be said. All of these means of Christian growth are significant. And they are all things of which we are aware. It is the matter of doing it, of getting with it. We can never grow in these ways and through these means unless we start practicing them. Inscribed on many soft drink bottles are the words "No deposit, No return." How true this is. Without any deposit there cannot be any return. Many of us are not getting any return because we are not making any deposit. Remember, the section began by saying that a *willing* head is a part of the preparation for discipleship.

A Willing Hand

Service is always a part of Christian discipleship. With these new believers in Acts 2 it took the form of having all things in common. They were each so willing to participate in the life and needs of the others that they did not consider their possessions their own. They willingly sold things, either personal or real property, in order to help the others. This was not established as a permanent form for Christians. Deception and discrimination entered in and soon this particular form was abandoned. What was not abandoned, however, was the need of Christian service. What was not abandoned either, was the need of sharing in ways we can, both our lives and our goods, with others.

We can think of it in several terms.

One abiding thought is that of mission. As Christians we are always on mission. There is never a time when a Christian is off duty. His duty is always to be on mission for his Savior.

This demands from us a sensitivity to others and to their needs. It will mean that we seek to be observant about the ways that we can help others. It was this attitude that led the late Frank Laubach, the literary missionary, to write, "It would be better for us to throw away ninety-nine per cent of our learning and of our tangled philosophy and stick to just one simple thing in our daily life—to keep asking God, 'Who needs me next, Father?' " [3]

And we also think in terms of ministry. The ministry that we provide to others is providing also to Jesus according to his parable of the judgment in Matthew 25.

Ministry does not have to be spectacular. It does need to be done in the name of Christ and for the good of others. It can be as unspectacular as that very needed ministry performed by one of the men in our church. A retired Baptist minister who is a member of our church has suffered a stroke. Even though he is partially paralyzed and cannot speak at all, he has been kept at home. Each night this fellow Christian goes to his home to put him to bed. Each morning he goes there to get him up, bathe him, and prepare him for the day. There is not a great deal about those necessary acts that is spectacular. But, there is a lot about them that is Christian. The willing hand that serves in Christian discipleship is willing to turn its hand in just such ministering acts.

Witness is a part of our Christian service. Having been forgiven of our sins by the Savior we have a compulsion to witness to others about what God has done in Jesus Christ and what he can do for them. This witness can be incidental and by the way as well as planned and structured.

In his book, *Angels: God's Secret Agents,* Billy Graham told the story of John Harper's last convert. John Harper was a passenger on the *Titanic*. Weighing 46,000 tons, that great ship was considered unsinkable. On the night of April 14, 1912, while cruising through the ocean at twenty-two knots it struck an iceburg. Because it did not carry enough life preservers or lifeboats 1,513 people drowned when it sank.

John Harper was on his way to Chicago to preach at Moody Church. Trying to stay afloat in the ocean he drifted toward a young man holding onto a plank. Harper asked him, "Young man, are you saved?" The man said, "No." A wave separated them. After a few minutes they drifted within speaking distance of each other. Again Harper called to him, "Have you made your peace with God?" The young man said, "Not yet." A wave overwhelmed John Harper and he was seen no more, but the words, "Are you saved?" kept ringing in the young man's ears.

Two weeks later a youth stood up in a Christian Endeavor meeting in New York, told his story, and said, "I am John Harper's last convert.'' [4]

This kind of witnessing style, the willingness to bear witness to Christ even while losing one's life, is the witness of the faithful disciple. It means being faithful even to the end.

Preparation is essential for discipleship. While we willingly prepare for so many other things, we often leave the development of our Christian discipleship entirely to chance. This must not be. With a willing heart to accept Christ, a willing head to learn of him, and a willing hand to serve him we can embark on the continuing process of preparing for discipleship.

4

The Dedication of Discipleship

Following the election of John F. Kennedy as president of the United States in 1960, Theodore White wrote the first of his series of "The Making of the President" books. It was entitled *The Making of a President: 1960*. In this book he sought to find the factors that went into John F. Kennedy's amazing capture of the presidency in that year.

One of the factors isolated by White was the existence of a vast grassroots organization that worked for Kennedy. In each state, county, and city there were any number of volunteers who gave of themselves and their time to bring about his election. Many of these people were never known to him. Their names were not recorded for posterity. They received little recognition. But they worked with dedication. Because of their dedicated work their candidate was elected president.

To function properly, or to succeed, any movement or organization must have people who work silently and efficiently behind the scenes.

The political campaign would never be a success without them. The great industries would not move if were it not for the men in the blue-collared shirts who turn up for work each day.

The work of the Lord is not different. The preachers are seen and heard constantly. The Sunday School teachers make their appearance each Sunday. The people of the church are acquainted with the church officers. But there also must be that person whose name might not be so prominently known who works quietly, regularly, efficiently, and with dedication. Without him the kingdom of God would not progress.

The best biblical example of this kind of dedicated disciple is Andrew. He is not mentioned many times in the New Testament. And when he is, it is usually in relation to his brother, Simon Peter. He was identified as "Andrew, the brother of Simon." But he had a tremendous role to play.

In *Mr. Jones, Meet the Master* Peter Marshall suggested that Andrew is the quiet, unassuming everyday Christian. He might be the man next door, the milkman, or the barber. He does not make much copy for the newspaper, but he is the man who supplies the copy. He might not make much show of his Christianity. But he is solid to the core. He is the dedicated disciple.

Sure, we need outspoken men like Peter. But we also need the quieter men like Andrew. We need the people who are seen up front. But we also need the people who work behind the spiritual scenes.

From at least three places in the New Testament we can gain a glimpse of Andrew which allows us to see that he is a good case study for the dedication of discipleship. Through the dedication of Andrew in his service with the Savior we can see something of what the dedication of discipleship would demand from us.

Recognition

The dedicated disciple recognizes the claims of Jesus.

Among those claims is his claim to messiahship.

One of the first glimpses we get of Andrew is in the company of John the Baptist. The story is told in John 1:35-42. While with John the Baptist, Andrew saw Jesus pass. And he heard John say, "Behold the lamb of God!" (John 1:36). When John gave this designation, Andrew recognized Jesus as the Messiah—God's promised one.

Andrew was one of the first to recognize this claim of Jesus and to follow him. This quiet man had such faith that he was able to see in Jesus the fulfillment of God's promise. It did not take repeated visits to convince him. It did not take a great deal of pleading or clever arguments for him to understand. He was not the object of repeated prayers over a long period of time. He simply heard the claim of the Christ, recognized it as valid, and followed him.

When I was younger, I often wondered if my salvation was as valid as some other people's salvation. After all, I had not been claimed from a sordid life of sin and ruin. When I heard some of the great and thrilling testimonies of God's grace in saving some of those characters, I wondered if my own salvation were worth as much as theirs.

There was one man who lived on my newspaper route as a twelve-year-old who was drunk the first time I met him. I was trying to collect the several weeks back subscriptions that he owed me. He offered to roll the dice with me to determine which of us paid his subscription. I declined to settle the debt that way. He soon moved from my route.

The next time I saw that man he was the leader in our high school Church Training group at church. Between the two times that I had just described he had found Christ as his Savior. And he liked to tell about it. At each opportunity, he was eager to give his testimony of God's grace. And it was thrilling. But I recall one time after he had given his story of salvation our pastor remarked that it takes as much of God's grace to save an individual and keep him from that kind of life of sin as it does to save a person from that kind of life. That helped me then. And it has helped me since.

The thrilling stories of salvation from terrible sin show the grace of God. But it takes no less faith, no less commitment, no less of God's grace for one to simply and quietly recognize Christ's claims and accept him as Savior.

When one recognizes the claim of Jesus as Savior, he will also recognize the claim of Jesus to his life. In Mark 1:17 Jesus again met Andrew. Likely this was after his first encounter with him described in John 1. At this time Jesus said to him, "Follow me and I will make you become fishers of men" (RSV). Jesus has the first claim upon our lives.

He may not ask each of us to leave our occupation to follow him as he did Andrew and Peter. But he will ask us to glorify our occupation through following him. Recognizing the claim of Christ to our lives we will also recognize that he would enable us to use our occupation as a point of contact and a means of entry for Christian witness.

This would also indicate that we would recognize the claim of Jesus to urgency. There is some significance to the fact that when Jesus called these early disciples to follow him, "Immediately they left their nets and followed him" (Mark 1:18, RSV). This is not the only place in the Scriptures that one has noticed the urgency of the command of God to him. When the book of Hosea described the action of the prophet Hosea, it records that "The Lord said to Hosea, 'Go' So he went" (Hos. 1:2-3, RSV). And when Isaiah had his great experience in the temple he said, "And I heard the voice of the Lord saying, 'Whom shall I send, and who will go for us?' Then I said, 'Here I am! Send me' " (Isa. 6:8, RSV).

It is tremendously urgent that we hear Christ's claim, accept him, and take our stand for him as disciples who would follow him. At almost any stage we can think of reasons that it can be put off until a later time. The child will want to wait until he is a young person. The young person might think that he needs to complete his education or begin his own home. The young adult feels that he has to make a place for himself in the world. And the older adult is willing for the younger people to work for Christ. But the fact remains that each person must recognize the urgency with which the claim of Christ as Savior comes to our lives. It is a claim upon which we must act.

Introduction

As we look at the dedicated disciple we discover that the dedicated disciple will introduce others to Jesus. When one has met Jesus himself and has discovered the joy of salvation he will want to share that discovery with others.

The dedicated disciple introduces members of his own family to Jesus. In John 1 it was noted that Andrew was one of the first to recognize the claims of Jesus. Also, it should be noted that he wasted no time in introducing his brother Simon to Jesus. In John 1:41-42 these words are found, "He [Andrew] first found his brother Simon, and said to him, 'We have found the Messiah (which means Christ). He brought him to Jesus" (RSV).

Some interpreters feel that means that Andrew found his brother Simon before John, who was also with him, found his brother James. I would rather believe that it means that the first thing that Andrew did was to find his brother Simon and tell him about Jesus.

Our first responsibility is for those persons who are nearest to us. But this is also our most difficult responsibility. It is much easier to talk to someone who does not know you about the meaning of Jesus than it is to talk to those who know you well about the power of Jesus in a human life.

When a person is unconcerned about those that are nearest to him, it represents a great tragedy in Christian faith. I was twenty years of age when I was called to my first pastorate in a rural church in central Louisiana. I had been taught that you need to know the prospects for membership to grow a church. And I also knew that the only way to know the prospects was to take a census. So I proposed a census of that rather large church field.

On the Sunday afternoon for the census four other persons turned up to help me take it. They lasted that one afternoon. But I was determined that the census would be taken. On Saturday and Sunday afternoons for weeks I labored until the census was completed. And it was one of the best things I ever did, because it helped me to know the community well.

One Sunday afternoon I drove into a yard where a man was working on a car, underneath a shade tree. I introduced myself, chatted with him a few minutes, then proceeded with the business at hand. He was a section foreman with a railroad. Readily he gave me the names and ages of every member of his family. But when it came to Christian profession and church affiliation he could give me no information beyond his own. Was it any wonder that none of the children then living at home were members of any church or Sunday School? This story has a happy ending though. Through the years I keep running into members of that family who are active members now.

But the dedicated disciple also introduces others to Jesus. This shows up in Andrew's actions in two other places. In John 6 when Jesus fed the five thousand men with a little boy's lunch of five loaves and two fishes it was Andrew who located the boy and introduced him to Jesus. In John 12:20 when some Greeks turned up inquiring about Jesus it was Andrew who took them to Jesus. They had first asked Philip, who had a Greek name, and Philip took them to Andrew who took them to Jesus. Apparently Andrew was in the habit of introducing other people to Jesus.

The dedication of discipleship shows in the way a person can naturally and normally introduce others to his Savior. It does not have to be a big production; it does need to be a sincere and natural introduction.

When I was growing up, there was a railroad conductor who lived next door to us. Everyone in the neighborhood loved him. But he was not a professing Christian. One night he went to a high school football game with my father and me. After the game we pulled the car up in the backyard under a tree and my father very simply and very sincerely explained to his neighbor his relationship to Christ and asked him to make a similar decision. Is it any wonder that I had trouble understanding the father described earlier? And is it any wonder that this is one of my finest memories of my Baptist deacon father?

D. L. Moody was once asked how Christians could reach the masses with the gospel. He replied that it could be done by going after them one by one. This method has never changed. But for it to be done dedicated disciples will need to introduce others to the Christ.

Acknowledgement

The dedication of discipleship also carries with it an acknowledgement. It is the acknowledgement that Jesus Christ is sufficient to meet all of our needs.

In Andrew's life this acknowledgement shows up very clearly in the incident of Jesus feeding the five thousand men. One of the records of this event is in John 6:1-14.

Included in this is the acknowledgement that Jesus can see and know our needs. As Jesus taught the people on the eastern shore of the Sea of Galilee he realized that they were hungry and in need. They had followed him around the end of the lake as he had gone across in a boat. They were a long way from home. They were unprepared. And they were hungry. Jesus knew their need.

We have come a long way when we can acknowledge that Jesus knows our needs. We may not even be totally aware of the needs that we have before Christ. The needs that grow out of our own feelings of self-sufficiency or self-satisfaction may be somewhat obscured in our own minds. But as we open ourselves to God in prayer and carry all of the needs of our lives to him then we can know that Jesus does know our needs as he knew the needs of those hungry people that day.

But involved in this also is the acknowledgement that Jesus is sufficient to meet those needs that we have. Philip wondered what could be done. Even though he was a native of the general area he could come to no solution as to how the people could be fed. Andrew knew that Jesus could do it.

Likely Andrew himself was not convinced of how Jesus could sufficiently meet that need. He just had the faith that he could. As he presented the boy with the lunch to Jesus, he indicated that there was some food available in the boy's lunch, but then he said, "But what are they among so many?" (John 6:9, RSV).

Even a little in the hands of Jesus is enough. Having the people sit down in rows, Jesus blessed this little lunch then distributed it to the people. And it was sufficient to meet their needs!

Even though Andrew was not quite sure how Jesus would work to make his sufficiency known among those people, he never wavered in his understanding that Jesus could. We are not always able to see beforehand how God will act. Would it be faith if we could understand it all before it happens? But in looking back over a life or over certain events we can have the assurance that Christ is truly sufficient to meet our needs that we bring before him.

And we would acknowledge that Jesus uses us and our efforts to meet these human needs. It was Jesus who fed the people. But it was Andrew who located the boy with the lunch and who brought him to Jesus. The focus of the miracle must be on Jesus. It was through his power that the miracle occurred. The miracle could never have happened in this way if Andrew had not brought the boy and his lunch to the Savior.

It is God who saves and it is God who strengthens. But God could not save if a person has not heard the gospel in witness through another person. And God cannot strengthen if that person is not brought to him and has no reminder from another that God's grace is truly sufficient for our every need.

It is much like the church which had gathered for prayer. As one of the deacons prayed, he prayed that God would provide some food for a family. Later in the prayer he returned to the food and told the Lord not to worry about that, he would take the food to them. God provided the food for that needy family. But he did it through a disciple who was willing to join his effort with God's in meeting a need.

Through the efforts of others, of us, people can see their places in God's work. They can see how God can work in their lives. We become enablers for God's power to be known.

The dedication of discipleship is much needed. It may not be the spectacular kind of service that calls attention to itself and is praised by other people. But without it the kingdom of God could never progress and the church of God could never function.

Perhaps it is best summarized in the familiar poem by Edgar A.

Guest, "Sermons We See."

I'd rather see a sermon than hear one any day,
I'd rather one should walk with me than merely show the way.
The eye's a better pupil and more willing than the ear;
Fine counsel is confusing, but example's always clear;
And the best of all the preachers are the men who live their creeds,
For to see the good in action is what everybody needs.
I can soon learn how to do it if you'll let me see it done.
I can watch your hands in action, but your tongue too fast may run.
And the lectures you deliver may be very wise and true;
But I'd rather get my lesson by observing what you do.
For I may misunderstand you and the high advice you give,
But there's no misunderstanding how you act and how you live.[1]

5

The Service of Discipleship

In *The Price Tags of Life,* C. Roy Angell passed on an interesting legend of creation. According to this legend, at the time of the creation of the world four angels approached God. Each of them asked a question.

The first angel asked, "How are you creating the world?" The question of the second angel was, "Why are you creating the world?" The third question was, "May I have it when you finish?" And the fourth angel's question was, "Can I help?"

Each of these questions is a good question. The first angel's question was the scientist's question. Through all these years the scientists have bent over their test tubes and searched their theories trying to answer the question "how." The second question is the philosopher's question. It is not confined to the university professors of philosophy. Each one of us has wondered why God created the world and the people of it. The third question is the epitome of selfishness. While we may be ashamed of that question, we also know that many of us spend a whole lifetime building a fence around a little part of this earth and some nations persistently try to rule the world. The fourth question, "Can I help?" is the Christian's question. It is born of the Spirit of Christ. And we can remember Paul trembling before the resurrected Christ asking, "Lord, what wilt thou have me to do?" (Acts 9:6).

We all like to help those we love. Sometimes, like children, our help is not very helpful or even needed, but we like to give it a try anyway.

Service is a part of Christian discipleship. As we follow Jesus, whose life was a life of service, we quickly recognize that we, too, must serve. How can we serve as disciples?

Turn to Mark's account of the arrest of Jesus in the garden of Gethsemane in Mark 14:43-52. As you read this, you have the same impulse of wanting to help Jesus. As Jesus was betrayed by Judas and was delivered into the hands of the arresting crowd you rather strain forward in the reading of it. "Isn't there anything that can be done?" you ask. And, then, as you read the passage again, you realize that efforts were made, futile though they were, to help Jesus in that time.

It is interesting to note the reaction of the disciples at that time of Jesus' greatest need. They had slept while Jesus had prayed. Even though he tried to forewarn them of this betrayal and arrest they had never quite understood. Then the hour arrived. They reacted by stark horror and terror. They ran and left him there. One of them, identified by John as Peter, tried to run them off with a sword and missed only severing the ear of a servant.

Reduced to its simplest form, the service of discipleship is helping Jesus. When we serve, we help Jesus; when we help Jesus, we serve as disciples.

Tragically our own efforts at helping Jesus often seem just as misguided and feeble as did those of the first disciples at his arrest. True, we want to help Jesus. That is what Christian service is. But how can I help Jesus? That is an important question as we think about the service of discipleship. From this experience of the earliest disciples we can begin to find an answer.

Negative: Some Things Do Not Help Jesus

As we begin to examine the service of discipleship we have to first look at it negatively. Some things we do may not help Jesus. They are not the elements of which Christian discipleship are made. Some of those very things are seen in the reactions of the disciples at the time of Jesus' arrest.

We do not help Jesus by betrayal. Judas betrayed his master. That was hardly a positive, helpful thing to do. We have given Judas a hard time because of his act of betrayal. And there is no way that his betrayal can be defended.

But we also betray the Christ. He is betrayed when we do not live up to Christian standards. He is betrayed when our lives contradict rather than confirm the gospel. He is betrayed when we seek to follow our own will rather than his will. He is betrayed when we confess love but live by a stifling legalism. He is betrayed when we affirm that salvation comes through faith then act as though it were maintained by works. In so many sly and insidious ways we have betrayed Christ and the principles of his life.

If we do not help Jesus by betrayal, neither do we help him by cowardice. The disciples stood before the arresting mob with quaking fear. They expressed cowardice before those who had come to arrest Jesus.

The spirit of fear is not the spirit that was given to us by Christ. When the disciples were afraid as the storm quickly churned up the Sea of Galilee when they crossed it in a boat Jesus contrasted fear and faith. He asked them, "Where is your faith?" (Luke 8:25, RSV).

Paul assured young Timothy that the spirit of fear was not one of the things God gave to him. Notice: "For God hath not given us the spirit of fear; but of power, and of love, and of a sound mind" (2 Tim. 1:7). From whatever source comes a spirit of fear, it does not come from Christ.

But this kind of fearful cowardice often marks the one who claims to serve Christ. At a time when Christians need to stand for Christian convictions, for justice for all persons, for sound government, for a moral consciousness in personal behavior, entertainment, and literature we have too often remained silent. It is not that the Christians have nothing to say. It is instead that they are fearful of expressing their thoughts due to the reaction they might receive.

And we do not help Jesus by retreat. The scriptural account sadly records, "And they all forsook him, and fled" (Mark 14:50). At the time when Jesus most needed the help and the strengthening presence of his friends, they retreated.

An interesting sidelight shows up in Mark 14:51-52 where it describes the young man who was present at the arrest wrapped in a linen cloth. When they grabbed him, he streaked off leaving his linen cloth behind. It can be assumed that this young man was Mark himself. The Last Supper had been at his mother's house. It was from there that Judas left when he left the group. That was probably the first place he went in looking for Jesus when he returned with the mob. Mark may have already gone to bed. Hearing the arresting crowd, he may have slipped out of bed and wrapped himself in his bedsheet to go and warn Jesus, but got there at about the time the crowd did. It may have been his way of saying that he was there. But he retreated also.

The direction of Christian service is forward. We are promised that we will never be left nor forsaken. And Jesus assured us that he would be with us to the very end, even the end of the age. So we should hardly be retreating at the sight and sound of some opposition to Christian principles or programs.

One of the most significant verses in all of the Scriptures is found in 1 Corinthians 16:9. There Paul said, "For a wide door for effective work has opened to me, and there are many adversaries" (RSV). With the opportunity came opposition. But the opposition can serve to stir us onward to greater determination and dedication to complete the task. Retreating from the opposition and leaving Christ's work and witness to fend for itself is never the answer.

We do not help Jesus by violence. Violence was one of the methods used to help Jesus when he was arrested. But it was unsuccesful.

It has been said that when Clovis the Frank first heard the gospel story as he was told about the crucifixion he jumped up, grabbed his sword, and said, "If I and my Franks had been there they would not have done that!"

It was this same attitude that was expressed by the man mentioned in Mark 14:47 who is identified in John's Gospel as Simon Peter. Peter was going to help Jesus by violently protecting him. He was not successful in that attempt. Swinging at the first person in sight, he cut off the ear of the high priest's servant. And you can be sure that he was not aiming at the ear. Perhaps he missed. Or perhaps the man moved his head and Peter only hit him with a glancing blow.

Violence has never been the way to advance the cause of Christ. In the Old Testament the kings and judges often tried violence. They were going to bring in the kingdom of God by violence. It did not work then, and it will not work now. Whether the violence is physical violence that attempts to force people to faith or verbal violence that abuses people or embarasses them or manipulates them or shames them or whether it is a method that violates the integrity of the individual, violence does not advance Christ's cause.

These are negative things that do not help Jesus. We observe that these were the reactions of the first followers of Christ at a time that he needed help. Contemporary followers of Jesus know that these attempts at service are only self-defeating. We do not help Jesus like that.

Positive: Faithfulness

If these negative ways do not help Jesus, how can we help Jesus? How can we serve him? In a word, by faithfulness. Since disciple-ship is following Jesus and being good at the things at which he was good, then the service of discipleship is being faithful to Jesus in all things.

Faithfulness begins now. Even though each person can likely think of some reason why it is better for him to put off being faithful to Jesus, it starts now. When Jesus was arrested in the garden of Gethsemane, he needed some people who were faithful to him then, not at some time in the future.

Every Christian generation faces a crisis of faith. Every Christian generation is called upon to express its faith in God at that time, not at some other time. And these crises never come upon us with advance warning. If we are not prepared for them when they come, we will never be prepared for them. It is likely that if the disciples had been forewarned and told that Jesus would be arrested that night in the garden of Gethsemane they would have prepared themselves for it. But it came suddenly; they had no time for further preparation. And since they were not previously prepared for faithfulness they were not faithful at the time when that was needed most.

Faithfulness starts now. We must accept Jesus now, just as we are, and follow him in faithfulness beginning now, just as we are. According to one of the versions of the story, there was a large gathering of noted people in London among whom was Caesar Milan, a noted preacher of his day. A young lady played and sang charmingly and everyone was delighted. Very graciously, tactfully, and yet boldly the preacher went up to her after she had performed and told her that he thought as he listened to her how tremendously the cause of Christ would be benefited if her talents were dedicated to his cause. He went on to say that she must realize that she was as much a sinner in the sight of God as a drunkard or a harlot. But, he added, that he was glad to tell her that the blood of Jesus Christ, the Son of God, would cleanse her from her sin.

She was offended and snapped out a rebuke for his presumption. His reply was that he meant no offense; he promised that he would pray that God's spirit would convict her, and that God would accept her if she came to him, just as she was.

They all returned to their homes. The young woman retired, but could not go to sleep. The face of the preacher appeared before her and his words continued to go through her mind. At two o'clock in the morning she got up from her bed, took a pencil and paper, and with tears dripping from her face, Charlotte Elliott wrote that famous song:

Just as I am, without one plea,
But that thy blood was shed for me,
And that thou bidd'st me come to thee,
O Lamb of God, I come! I come!

Faithfulness in the service of Jesus continues in great stress. It was during the time of stress that the first disciples forsook Jesus and fled. They had been proud to be with him when the crowds followed him in Galilee. And they had been pleased to accompany him in the triumphal entry into Jerusalem. But in that time of stress they departed from him.

The very nature of faithfulness demands that it continue in the times of great stress. If it cannot continue during stress, it is not faithfulness. There is no place for the summer soldier and the sunshine patriot in the service of Jesus.

Faithfulness in Christian service always rests in calm assurance in God. One of the most striking things of all about the account of the arrest of Jesus is that Jesus was the calmest one of all. The rest reacted violently, quaked in fear, ran in cowardice, or threatened with swords and staves. And in the midst of it all, very calmly, Jesus asked why they came after him armed so. If they had really wanted to take him, they could have done it any day as he taught in the Temple area.

Jesus was able to act with such calm because he had assurance in God. He had already prayed the matter through. He knew in his own heart that he would not be delivered from the cross. He would drink the cup of suffering and sacrifice down to the last dregs. But through all of that, he met it with assurance in God.

In many Indian tribes the boys faced a vigil of a night alone in the woods as a part of their rite of passage from boyhood into manhood. In one particular case the son of the chief received the same training as all the other boys. He too, went through the vigil of the night alone in the woods. He crouched near his fire as, just beyond the circle of the light cast by the fire, he could hear the movement of the wild animals of the night. Even though he could not see them he could hear them and his imagination worked more actively with each sound. But neither could he see that just beyond the circle of light also stood his father, the chief, with bow and arrow drawn, to make sure that nothing would harm his son. God always stands ready to help us in our time of need. We can have that assurance in God.

The service of discipleship is helping Jesus. Some things that we do may not actually help him. They may, instead, bring harm and reproach to the whole Christian cause. But by faithfulness to him throughout all of life we serve the best.

My daughter was four years old when one fall Saturday I raked some of the fallen pecan leaves in the front yard of our house. Then, after raking the leaves, I got a broom and began sweeping the long front porch. While I was sweeping, she came to the porch with the rake and was raking the front porch. I suggested to her that she should not rake the porch since that would scratch it and that she ought to just leave that little job to me. She left the porch and walking along the sidewalk dragging the rake behind her I heard her say, "I helping Jesus."

Somewhere along the way she had learned that when a little girl helps her daddy she is helping Jesus. And, as disciples of Jesus Christ, we know that when we are helping Jesus in the many ways that we can we are engaging in the service of discipleship.

6

The Behavior of Discipleship

Many of the demands that are made of us, and many of the opportunities that are ours, come because of who we are. J. Wallace Hamilton told of a father who, one September morning, went with his son to Grand Central Station in New York City. The son was taking the train for a college in New England. Just for a moment the father stood there, wanting to say so many things, but saying only one, though it was quite enough: "Bill, never forget who you are." Worth more than a book of rules or a score of lectures on behavior was that one challenge to something deep in a boy's remembrance. "Never forget who you are." The basis of behavior was the boy's own identity.

That is the basis of the plea which Paul made to the Christians at Philippi in Philippians 1:27-30 and through them to us: "Only let your conversation be as it becometh the gospel of Christ. . . ." Paul is saying, "In the way you act, remember who you are." In the seventeenth century, when the King James Version of the Bible was translated, "conversation" was much broader than it is used today. We use it in reference to our talk; it was then used in reference to the whole way or manner of life.

How is a disciple of the Lord Jesus Christ to behave? Is the behavior of discipleship any different from the behavior of any other individual?

I have asserted that, basically, Christian discipleship is following

Jesus. If this is true, then the behavior of the Christian disciple finds its basis in its confirmation with the life, teachings, and behavior of Jesus Christ, our Savior.

The apostle Paul has given to us, then, a plea for Christian behavior and it is based on our identity as citizens of the kingdom of God, on who we are. The New Testament has some startling descriptions of who we are. We are called "sons of God," "sons of light," "temples of the living God," and here in Philippians, colonists of the Christian commonwealth.

You will notice how this fits in with what has preceded. When Paul reported that the result of his imprisonment was that the gospel was being preached, he said that his goal in life was to magnify Christ, whether in life or in death. That suggested to him the dilemma that he faced—whether to die and go directly into the presence of Christ or to stay and minister in the name of Christ. He was confident, though, that he would live to see the Philippians again. Then he made his plea to them. Whether he ever saw them again, he pled for Christian behavior. And this is based on who they were: citizens of God's kingdom. The behavior of discipleship is based on who we are: disciples of Jesus.

What is involved in worthy Christian behavior?

Consistency

The first fact of the disciple's behavior is that it should be consistent with the gospel of Christ. This word *worthy* can also have the idea of "weighty." The Christian life then is to give weight to the Christian gospel.

The consistency of Christian behavior should mean that the life of a Christian would confirm rather than contradict the gospel. When we look at the gospel of Jesus Christ, we see some important elements: love, mercy, concern, forgiveness, the worth of the individual before God, hope. In our manner of life, we, as Christians, must be careful to see that these things are displayed. Our lives must be marked with these same elements if they are to be consistent with the gospel of Jesus Christ.

A rather strange and unusual word is used to express this idea. For the word that is translated "conversation," Paul used a word that meant actually "citizen life." This could have special meaning to the Philippians. Philippi was a colony of Rome. A Roman colony was treated exactly as though it were a part of Rome. The Roman colonies were little bits of Rome planted throughout the world. The people used the Latin language, wore Roman dress, and insisted on being stubbornly Roman. To these people who were conscious and proud of their identity as Romans, Paul appealed to a higher identity, that of being Christians.

As Christians we belong to a colony of heaven that is located on the earth. This demands that our lives be consistent with the principles upon which the colony was founded—the gospel of Christ.

Carl Sandburg was a devoted student of Abraham Lincoln. He was called to give the commencement address to a graduating class at Harvard University. It was at a time when another war was shaping up and young college men were confused, baffled, and some of them bitter. Sandburg thought of Lincoln who carried the weight of the terrible choices in his own heart. In his quiet, mystic way Sandburg said to that class that he thought they needed the spirit of prayer and humility of Abraham Lincoln who, in the "divided house" of his day, knew what to do because he knew who he was.

In Christian behavior we know who we are. We are followers of Jesus Christ. Therefore, we know what to do. Our lives, our actions, our attitudes, our stance toward things—in short, our behavior—must be consistent with the gospel.

Constancy

The behavior of discipleship is not only to be consistent with the gospel of Jesus Christ, it is also to be constant. "Stand fast" is the admonition of Paul to these Christian people. "Stand fast" in the face of awful and many and varied temptations from the world, the flesh, and the devil. Christian behavior is not a seasonal thing, it is to be a constant thing.

How are we to stand fast? How are we to be constant in the behavior of discipleship?

Constancy demands one spirit. It is by the Holy Spirit of God that we are to find the strength and the ability for constancy in the face of all the demands and all the strains. In him we find the strength of steadfastness. In him we are to discover the secret of unity. In him we have the sense of unfractured fellowship.

We soon realize that we are not developing Christian virtues in a vacuum. We are living in a world of sin and selfishness and greed. People are asserting themselves and screaming for their "rights" and their "place." The people with whom we deal in daily life are not always Christians. And many times they are making no effort to develop the pattern of Christian behavior in their own lives. They may even interpret it as a sign of weakness in the lives of others. To live as a Christian disciple and to behave as a Christian disciple in the face of such pressures demands dependence upon the Holy Spirit. This we cannot do on our own.

Constancy demands one mind—unity. You will notice that this constancy is not only with one spirit, but also with one mind. We must face the world with the unity of purpose and unity of faith that comes from our common faith in Christ. The church can never win the world when it itself is divided, fussing and bickering over minor points of procedure and policy. The church begins to make strides in its purpose of witnessing and ministering when it faces the world with one mind, with unity.

This "one mind" shows how we will work "striving together for the faith of the gospel" (Phil. 1:27). Our word *athlete* is derived from one part of the word translated "striving." Now if there is anything that is needed on the athletic field it is teamwork; a group of people playing on a team possessing unity. The best teams are not those with one or two outstanding stars who carry all the load, but those that have balance and all the members share in the work. And this is absolutely necessary for constancy in Christian behavior.

In those ancient days when I was an elementary school student, one of the items marked on our report card was "conduct." Each six weeks, along with our grades for spelling, arithmetic, geography, history, and English, we were graded for our conduct.

I well remember one grading period when I took home a report card with a *C* in conduct. I do not remember what the particular problem was. I do remember that several of my pals and I received a *C* in conduct. And I do remember my mother's reaction to it. My mother was not too well pleased with a *C* in anything. She took an extremely dim view of a *C* in conduct. She told me something like this: "I don't expect you to be smart. I don't care if you don't make all *A*'s. But I do expect you to behave yourself. I do expect you to make an *A* in conduct. Whether you can learn anything or not, you can behave yourself. And I expect you to do it. Whatever else you can do, you can behave."

And I rather suspect that our Lord expects that kind of constancy from us. He does not call us to be spectacular or super Christians. He does call us to be constant in following the principles of Christian behavior.

Courage

Courage is also a necessary ingredient of the behavior of discipleship. "And in nothing terrified by your adversaries" (Phil. 1:28), is the way Paul expressed it. That word for frightened means to be startled like a scared horse or fluttered like a surprised bird.

The Christian is to show courage in the face of persecution. The fact that they had adversaries indicates that some kind of persecution was at hand. The Christian always faces some persecution if it is nothing more than coolness and condescension from some of his more "worldly" friends.

In *The Adequate Man,* Paul Rees tells of a young Hindu who was bitterly censured by his family because he became a Christian. When he refused to renounce Christ, he was legally cut off from his share in the large family fortune. Later, the brothers and sisters fell to quarreling over the distribution of his share in the estate. They finally came to him and asked him if he would arbitrate their differences. They said that their reason for asking him was that he was the only one that all of them would trust.

The Christian is to show courage in the fact of suffering. Notice that suffering is not always an accident. Paul indicated that it was "given" to these Christians. This is the root word for grace. Suffering sometimes comes because of our own foolishness. But suffering sometimes comes to be used as a gift of God.

What is the result of all this? What can become of the Christian's courage in the face of persecution and the fact of suffering? It can be used to confound the adversaries of Christ and the doubters of Christianity. It becomes a token of salvation.

Harry Emerson Fosdick, in *What Is Vital in Religion,* related the incident of the black maid who worked in the home of the sculptor Gutzon Borglum. Each day, as she would clean the studio, she would notice chips of marble around a larger piece. One day she went into the study and saw a marble bust of Abraham Lincoln. She then asked Borglum how he knew Mr. Lincoln was in that stone.

In each one of us is the making of a courageous disciple of Jesus. As we pay attention to the behavior of discipleship as a part of the commitment we have to Christ, that disciple can emerge.

This is the meaning of the behavior of discipleship. Paul nowhere intimated that it would be easy. But it will be grand.

There is a French tale which tells how a French soldier came upon a young recruit trembling with fear in a desperate situation. "Come, son," said the veteran, "and you and I will do something fine for France."

That is exactly what we can do in Christian behavior. As disciples who follow Jesus Christ we can do something fine for our Lord. And we can do it by the way we behave ourselves, by the very way we live.

7

The Obligation of Discipleship

An obligation is something to which we are surely accustomed. In the days of the draft we spoke of the military obligation of the young man to his country. We speak of the financial obligations that we all feel—house payments, car payments, insurance premiums, and our other regular obligations. We speak of the obligations of citizenship—being informed, taking a part in government, voting. It should not strike us as strange, then, when we encounter the obligations of discipleship.

We have usually said that the Bible is a book of principles rather than rules. We are a little disappointed and taken back, then, when we read the demands placed on the Gentile converts in Acts 15. This sounds strangely like rules and regulations. We shall see, though, that these are also great underlying principles. Rather than the obligations of law, they are the obligations of love.

The problem that prompted the Jerusalem conference, which some have called the first ecumenical council, was what to do with the Gentile converts to Christianity. Christianity was at first confined to the Jews. Then the universal implication of the gospel was understood, missionary efforts and journeys were undertaken, and Gentiles began to be converted.

Then the Judaizers moved in. They were the people who believed that salvation came from faith in Jesus Christ *and* observing the Jewish law, especially the practice of circumcision.

This caused quite a concern among the Gentile Christians. Following Paul's first missionary journey they assembled a conference in Jerusalem to discuss the matter. At stake was the question of who could be a Christian.

Evidently there was much discussion at the conference. The account in Acts gives three distinct movements: Peter's argument, Paul and Barnabas' report, and James's summary and suggestion.

James carried the day. He was the leader of the Jerusalem church. His leadership was not so much that of an official office as it was a moral leadership due to his outstanding character. He was a brother of Jesus who had a special resurrection appearance. After that he became a believer. He was a pillar of the church. James was so constant in prayer that his knees were said to be as hard as a camel's because he knelt so often and so long. He was so good a man that he was called James the Just. But more importantly, he was a rigorous observer of the law. James came down on the side of the Gentiles. And it helped to carry the day.

The issue was settled. A person could become a Christian through faith in Jesus Christ. Nothing more was necessary. One did not have to become a Jew before he could be a Christian. All believers in Jesus Christ could be let into the fellowship of believers without hindrance.

But how would the Jewish and the Gentile Christians get along together? This also was at stake. Admittedly the Gentiles could become Christians, but could they have fellowship together? To make things easier James suggested certain obligations that the Gentile Christians should keep. They may seem a bit antiquated to us, but the principles show us our obligation as Christians. These suggestions were adopted and communicated to the Gentile Christians through a letter.

For us, as for these early Christians, it was an obligation of love rather than law. These obligations did not determine whether one could be a Christian. They did show how the Christians would relate to one another in love.

These same principles become our obligations of discipleship. These same issues keep cropping up before the contemporary Christian. Consider these obligations of discipleship.

An Uncompromising Purity

One obligation of Christian discipleship is an uncompromising purity. They were asked to "abstain . . . from unchastity" (Acts 15:29, RSV) or from fornication (KJV, NEB).

The truth is that Christianity brought into the world a new standard of sexual purity. Infidelity was common among both the Romans and the Greeks. Not only was it common, in many cases it was expected. Homosexuality was called the national disease of Greece. When you read Romans 1 and then read the accounts of the Roman historians, you realize that Paul has not overstated his case. The world was rife with sexual immorality. The very cities into which Paul had gone with the gospel, and in which churches had been established, were places where this kind of immoral sexual conduct was common.

This ran against the grain of Jewish ethics. But more importantly, it ran against the standards of Christian conduct. The Christian demand was that a man must keep himself "unstained from the world" (Jas. 1:27, RSV).

This is surely an obligation for the Christian in our day. In the face of the sexual revolution, the new morality, the relaxed standards, and the openness of discussion of sexual matters, the Christian has an obligation to uphold a purity of life.

The obligation begins with the scriptural teachings. The Ten Commandments have not yet become the Ten Suggestions. The Seventh Commandment unequivocally states, "Thou shalt not commit adultery" (Ex. 20:14). This does not speak of the extenuating circumstances, or the prevalence of the practice in your subdivision, or of the suggestiveness of the reading material. It rather pointedly indicates that the one who follows God should have an uncompromising regard for the institution of marriage and the importance of the person.

Jesus carried it a step further in the Sermon on the Mount. In Matthew 5:27-30 Jesus broadened the understanding of the Seventh Commandment to include sexual unchasity in general, and not just adultery by a strict definition. He also located its inward source. It often begins in the mind and the heart. When a person thinks on unchaste matters and feeds his mind on them, the act is less difficult when the opportunity is found.

This obligation is also based on the respect which you have for human personality. A person must be treated as a person and not a thing. No human being is simply an instrument of someone else's pleasure. Each person's integrity of personhood must be considered.

One of the interpretations of sex that needs correcting is that sex is simply another of the human appetites. They say that if it is another of the human appetites, like hunger, then it must be satisfied. Under this interpretation the sexual act is little more than satisfying a physical desire. But it is much more than that. It involves the whole person and it involves the whole personality. Because of this it must be treated with more respect.

Related to this is the matter of pornographic literature. The nation is swept with a flood of pornography. The filling of the mind with that kind of literature cannot create a Christian consciousness of purity and chastity. It is an immature kind of behavior that rests upon untrue presentations of persons. Healthy sexual attitudes and behavior can hardly result from that kind of material.

The Bible teaches that sex is good; it is neither evil nor dirty. It is a part of God's creation. And God pronounced his creation good.

But the Bible and the Christian conscience also teach that sexual activity should be confined to marriage. It helps to expand the marriage relationship. Outside of marriage it tends to harm the individual and to make it difficult for him to establish a lasting, loving, relationship in marriage.

Many of the problems that we face in our nation today—rising divorce rate, epidemic venereal disease, floods of pornography, absorption with sexual matters—could be treated if Christians took seriously their obligation for an uncompromising purity.

This whole obligation also rests upon the principle of prior commitment. The Christian has made a prior commitment of his life to Jesus Christ. He has made a prior commitment to the standards of Christian conduct. If he is married, he has made a prior commitment to his mate. If unmarried, he still has a commitment that he has made to Christ and to himself. Then when he is confronted with the particular situation he does not have to make a decision. He has already made that decision with his prior commitment.

Several years ago the *Reader's Digest* printed an article by a mother on sex education. It was entitled "What Shall I Tell My Daughters?" The concluding paragraph is worth repeating.

Phyllis McGinley said, "So what shall I tell my daughters about chastity before marriage. I shall be sensible and point out the social penalties attached to any other conduct. I shall touch on the possible pregnancy, the untidiness, the heartbreak. But I shall also say that love is never merely a biological act but one of the few miracles left on earth, and that to use it cheaply is a sin." [1]

An Uncompromising Loyalty

Another of the obligations of the Christian disciple is an uncompromising loyalty. The person who follows Jesus must be loyal to Jesus.

In the Acts account it shows up in the prohibition against eating meat that had been offered to idols. That is hardly a problem for us today. It was a real problem among the first-century Christians.

When sacrifices were made to the pagan idols, only a portion of the meat was consumed in the sacrifice. The remainder could be eaten by the worshipers. Often friends would be invited to share in these meals. For the Christian, then, to abstain from eating the meat that had been offered to idols was to make a clean break with paganism. He was also cutting off a great deal of his social life with non-Christians.

While the liberated Christian was convinced that the idol was not real and the meat was probably good, eating it could offend the conscience of the weaker Christian and indicate to some of the idol worshipers an acceptance of their god. So for the sake of loyalty to Jesus Christ the new believers were asked to abstain from eating that meat.

Something of the loyalty of those who had first preached Christ to the Gentiles was indicated in the phrase describing them in the letter to the Gentile Christians. They were, "Men that have hazarded their lives for the name of our Lord Jesus Christ" (Acts 15:26). This is the same kind of loyalty that we need to have for Jesus.

Ours is a day of diminishing loyalty. People do not often have a strong loyalty to anything. In spite of the bicentennial celebration patriotism is not running too deeply. Students do not have a real loyalty to their schools. People do not show an abiding loyalty to their friends or to the causes they have espoused. It is surely seen in the church. Many of the church members do not show a strong loyalty to the church and to its ministries.

In the face of the diminished loyalties seen all around us, the one who follows Jesus in Christian discipleship is called to an uncompromising loyalty.

Could it still be that we are called to hazard our lives for Jesus Christ in loyalty to him? Ask Georgi Vins in Russia. He has been persecuted along with other evangelical Christians for his uncompromising loyalty to Christ.

Ask the young man about whom I read from a non-Christian home who went to church and was converted. The pastor told him he would have a hard time at home if he lived for Christ. But he declared that he was willing to suffer anything for Jesus. The next Wednesday night the pastor started to pat him on the back. The boy drew back and asked the pastor not to touch him on the back. They then went to a room together and the boy pulled off his shirt. His back was bloody for his father had beaten him for becoming a Christian and joining the church.

But our loyalty may not be called into question in such radical ways. Remember that part of the problem of eating meat that was offered to idols centered in the social life. In subtle ways, in social gatherings or in business contacts or in commercial practices, we may compromise our loyalties to Jesus.

J. B. Gambrell once said that he would not have a dog that ran under another man's wagon. The Christian person must be loyal to Jesus Christ. He cannot live with divided loyalties.

Gambrell's statement made me think of a dog we once had. He was the neighborhood pet. Not only did he play with our children and eat our food, but he also had several stops up and down the street where he ate food and played with people. After awhile he got to disappearing. Sometimes he would be gone for two or three days at a time. We would get a call from someone at some distance saying that the dog was there. We would go get him to bring him back home. Not only was this aggravating, it was also disappointing. We wanted him to be our dog, our pet. We expected him to play with us, to watch our house, and to be our companion. While his divided loyalties may have made him popular, it did not display his love and loyalty to us. That was what we wanted. And that is what the Savior wants from those who claim his name.

Uncompromising Love

You will notice that another obligation of the Christian is for uncompromising love. The Gentile Christians were asked to abstain from blood and from things strangled. This is a reference to the Jewish dietary laws.

The Jewish dietary laws forbade them to eat meat that still had blood in it. So there were special ways of killing meat and draining the blood from the meat before it was eaten. This was what made it kosher.

It would not concern the Gentile Christians too much if their meat had not been properly bled. It would concern the Jewish Christians at table fellowship with them. To abstain from blood and from things strangled would indicate a willingness to show Christian charity toward others. It would be a willingness to compromise on a nonessential matter for the sake of fellowship.

This is Christian love in action.

Christian love shows a high regard for the other person. It is willing to take the other person's needs and feelings into consideration. It is willing to accept him as a person, for what he is.

In his biography of D. L. Moody, entitled *Moody,* J. C. Pollack told of a little boy who walked nearly three miles every week to Illinois Street where Moody conducted a Sunday School when there were Sunday Schools closer to his home. He was asked why he did that. His reply was, "They love a fellow over there."

When a fellow is loved and he knows that he is loved, he finds more self-worth. And he finds a fellowship that is satisfying and meaningful to him. Christian love tries to help persons find that kind of meaning and worth.

When you become concerned about the feelings and the fellowship of others you will be showing that love of Christ. In Eugene O'Neill's play, *The Great God Brown,* the central figure, Brown, lay dead on the street. A policeman bent over his body and asked his name. Someone replied that his name was "Man." Then the policeman with his notebook and pencil asked how it was spelled.

How do you spell man? Some have spelled man as "slave" or as "master." How you spell "man" will show in how you treat other persons, what you think of yourself, how you will show love to those persons who are both unloved and unlovely.

The missionary who leaves a potentially lucrative medical practice to practice medicine in the name of Christ shows how he spells "man." The teacher who cares deeply for his students tells how he spells "man." The person who volunteers his time to help in the hospital, with those who have abused chemical substances, or to minister in a nursing home with forgotten folks shows how he spells "man."

And the person who is so willing to show love that he will forsake his own "rights" for what is right shows that his love is motivated by

Christ.

There are any number of things that Jesus does not demand that we do. While he wants us to witness, he does not demand that we preach to thousands of persons. While he commended stewardship, he does not demand that we become Schweitzers or Luthers or Grahams. He does demand that we love.

The one distinguishing mark that Jesus gave for his disciples was that they love one another. And one way this love shows up is in the willingness to act in love toward others, taking into consideration their feelings and their tender conscience. Paul did that when he had Timothy circumcised so that this half-Jew, who had become a Christian, would not be offensive to the Jews to whom they would witness. Jesus did that when he willingly emptied himself and took on the role of a servant when he became a man. And the Christian does that when he limits his own liberty for the greater goal of an unobstructed witness to the Savior.

In commenting on self-imposed martyrdom, psychoanalyst Wilhelm Stekel once said, "The mark of an immature man is that he wants to die nobly for a cause, while the mark of the mature man is that he wants to live humbly for one." [2]

As disciples of Jesus Christ we are called to be mature persons. When we live nobly for him, there are certain self-imposed obligations. As we follow these obligations of love we indicate something of the measure of our discipleship.

8

Discipleship and Duty

Inscribed beneath the bust of Robert E. Lee in the Hall of Fame are these words: "Duty then is the sublimest word in the language. Do your duty in all things. You cannot do more. You should never do less."

Lee showed his commitment to that concept at the outbreak of the Civil War. Holding a commission as a United States Army officer, he resigned that commission to command the Army of Northern Virginia. Virginia, his native state, had become a part of the Confederacy. It was his duty to fight for his home and to fight with his people.

A sense of duty is a very important matter for any person. Daniel Webster once said, "A sense of duty pursues us forever. It is omnipresent like the Deity. If we take to ourselves the wings of the morning, and dwell in the uttermost parts of the sea, duty performed or duty violated is still with us, for our happiness or our misery. If we say the darkness shall cover us, in the darkness as in the light our obligations are yet with us."

Yet at the same time that we give credence to a sense of duty and the necessity of duty we realize that just to do our duty is not enough. Duty alone is not ample discipleship.

That is the point of a parable that Jesus told to his disciples as recorded in Luke 17:7-10. It is a parable that is found only in Luke and was directed to the disciples themselves. Preceding the parable are sayings about causing others to stumble and about forgiveness.

Then the disciples asked Jesus to increase their faith. His reply to them showed that faith was not so much a matter of quantity as quality. It was not the quantity of faith that needed increasing so much as the quality of faith. Right on the heels of this is the parable.

The parable deals with the stewardship of faith and the relation of duty to discipleship. Some would consider it a warning against pride in the amount of faith they had. Faith is not something to be rewarded. Faith is expected of the disciple. Faith is our duty. If we follow Jesus in Christian discipleship, then faith must be a part of our lives.

Jesus took a familiar picture from life in a rural area to illustrate it. After a servant, literally a slave, had spent the day plowing or keeping the sheep, he would not be rewarded by the master by being served by the master. Rather, he would be expected to come to the house and to prepare the meal and to serve the master before he got his own meal and rest. This part of service is a part of his duty.

The disciples got the point. They replied, "We are unworthy servants; we have only done what was our duty" (Luke 17:10, RSV). In other words, they were not worthy of special praise or special reward because they had just done their duty, nothing more.

As Christians we are not in for some kind of special award of merit because we practice discipleship. That is our duty. To be a Christian means to be a disciple. It is our duty to follow Jesus; it is our duty to live by faith; it is our duty to minister in his name and to witness for his sake.

We consider this matter when it comes to Christian stewardship. We have a duty to be faithful stewards, good administrators of the things that God has given to us. To practice stewardship does not call for special praise. As disciples who follow Jesus who gave his all, giving from our possessions is our duty.

But duty does not exhaust our responsibility. If we just "do our duty," we have not gone far into the real meaning of giving ourselves to Christ. Duty is a higher motive for giving than many motives. It is a higher motive than fear, for instance. But duty as the only motive can become dangerous. Robert J. Hastings in his book, *My Money and God,* said that duty alone can become cold, mechanical, and legalistic. That would degrade giving to the level of mere bill-paying.

In Christian service and ministry we quickly realize that duty is not enough. Often duty does not give us that personal expression of faithfulness, loyalty, and love that we need in Christian discipleship.

As disciples we have a duty. But there is more to true discipleship than simple duty.

Going Beyond Duty

Notice that in the parable the servant did not get any thanks or special reward for what he had done. He had simply done his duty as a servant. Our service to God, our attendance at worship services, our teaching of Sunday School classes, and our giving may be done out of a sense of duty. We do have a duty to God. But it must go beyond duty. It must include love.

Many people have served in a church with a sense of duty. Then when they considered that their duty had been done their service was terminated. Consider, for instance, the people who would work in Sunday School or with the youth groups as long as their children were involved in the programs. But when the children grew up or left home, suddenly their service to the Savior stopped. Their explanation was that they had done their duty. Let someone else serve now. Where is their love? Where is their devotion to Christ? Where is the concept of discipleship that demands that one would serve Christ simply because he follows Christ?

Discipleship demands that we go beyond duty and act out of love.

A building is burning and a child is trapped inside the building. For any number of reasons a fireman would not hesitate to go into the building, risking his life, as Robert J. Hastings once pointed out. He might act from duty, pride, self-respect, or loyalty. But there is no question about the mother of the child. She would not stop to think about duty or loyalty or pride or self-glory. She would not even stop to determine whether she could return alive. Love for her child would drive her into the burning building to attempt to rescue the child. While the fireman might act from duty, the mother would act from love. And which is the higher motive? Of course, love is the higher motive.

Because of love God sent his son, Jesus Christ, into our world to die for us. Again and again, we have quoted, "For God so loved" (John 3:16).

Having known and experienced the love of God, we should also act out of love. Mere duty is hardly enough for ministry, witness, and stewardship. Discipleship demands that we go beyond duty, to love.

In one of the post-resurrection appearances of Jesus, recorded in John 21, Jesus appeared before the earliest disciples while they were fishing. After directing their efforts to success, they came to the shore to breakfast with him. There he asked Simon Peter a decisive question. The question had one focus: the quality of Peter's love. Three times he asked, "Simon, son of John, do you love me?" (John 21:15-17, RSV). Each time the question brushed aside the irrelevancies that we would have thrown up—education, social standing, economic condition, status, prestige, leadership, accomplishments, and achievements—to get to the heart of the matter. Peter had denied Jesus in his hour of greatest need even though he had boasted that he would never forsake him. Duty had not carried Peter through. Did he love Jesus enough to be faithful to him?

It is when we look at the matter of love that we realize that we must surely go beyond duty. At the Southern Baptist Pastor's Conference in 1961, G. Earl Guinn made a telling point when he said that a man is not necessarily a saint because he attends all the meetings at the church. He might have a heart that is as hard as Pharaoh's and be as spineless as Pilate and as treacherous as Judas. Duty might get him to church. Only love can change his heart and truly motivate him for service.

So duty does not exhaust our relationship to God. It can never be explained just by a sense of duty. Duty must be overlaid by love. We cannot stop with duty; we must go beyond duty.

To Unreserved Obedience

Just as the slave owed unreserved obedience to his master, so do we owe unreserved obedience to God. Now this parable is not saying that God is like an exacting taskmaster, standing over us, always demanding more than we can give. Neither is it saying that we must have a slavish spirit in the things that we do for God. But it is telling us that as Christians, as disciples, we are servants of God who are called to unreserved obedience.

Just as a good citizen does not pick and choose which laws he will obey, and a good servant does not pick and choose which commands of his master he will obey, neither does the Christian disciple pick and choose in which areas he will be obedient to God. He must be absolutely and unreservedly obedient to God in all areas of life.

Consider what this does for us in the matters of self-satisfaction and pride. We can never be satisfied with our service to God. We can never have self-righteous pride in what we have done. We can never say that I have done this much and I will do no more; I have gone this far and I will go no farther. Someone once described Jesus as the unsatisfied shepherd. He was never satisfied with the number of sheep he had safely in the fold. And we can never be satisfied servants. We can never settle in with satisfaction that we have done all there is to be done for God. This is a part of our obedience to the master.

Rudolf Bultmann explained the ethic of Jesus as the ethic of radical obedience. In commenting on this parable he said that "it is absolutely clear that Jesus demanded obedience without any secondary motive. . . . For love with the secondary motive of reward, love with a backward look on one's own achievement, would not be love. Jesus' attitude is indeed paradoxical; he promises reward to those who are obedient without thought of reward." [1]

Acting out of obedience to God and to his will, without thought of the reward, we can be ministers in Christ's name. We can follow his guidance in where we serve, in how we serve, and to whom we serve.

In *All the Parables of Jesus,* Robert L. Cargill told of some Oklahoma Christians who were willing to help another person in obedience to Christ's command. They recognized a Christian duty. But more than duty called forth their action; it was obedience.

Just before Christmas, 1967, a Jewish man by the name of Daniel Bloomenthal came to the First Baptist Church of Altus, Oklahoma. He asked the church secretary if he could talk to the pastor. Gene Garrison, now pastor of the First Baptist Church, Oklahoma City, was then the pastor of the Altus church. He told Garrison that he had served five years in a New York prison and had been rejected by his family and people. He was sick with emphysema and was trying desperately to get to Phoenix, Arizona.

While hitchhiking near El Reno, Oklahoma, he was picked up by a man who brought him to Altus. He noticed that the driver had a fishhook in his coat lapel and asked its meaning. The man replied that he was glad he had asked that. The fishhook, he explained, meant that he was a follower of Jesus Christ and a fisher of men. He then proceeded to try to lead his passenger to the Lord. The Jewish passenger was cynical and unbelieving. The witnessing Christian seemed to make no headway. Arriving in Altus, the driver turned south toward Vernon, Texas, but said to his passenger who was continuing west, "Mr. Bloomenthal, you are cynical and unbelieving now, but someday you will be in serious trouble and find no one to help you. When this happens, go to a born-again Christian, and he will help you."

The hitchhiker said that he had tried to catch a ride for three hours. Then it occurred to him that he could drop dead and no one would care. To the pastor he said, "Reverend, that hurt me worse than anything in the world. I was beaten in prison, and another time I was beaten and left for dead in an alley in New York, but nothing ever hurt me so bad as to realize that no one cared."

Garrison then called three businessmen who were members of the church. They came to the office and heard the man's story. The man said that he was not promising anything. All that he knew was that he would die unless he could get some help. And he was desperate enough to take the advice of the man with the fishhook who had given him the ride.

Each of the three Christian businessmen took twenty dollars out of his billfold and handed it to Bloomenthal. Tears welled up in his eyes. He sat down and began to sob. After a few minutes he said that was the first time anyone had ever done anything for him with no strings attached. He did not think that anyone cared.

But someone did care. And those caring persons were able to follow with unreserved obedience in their help to another person. They moved beyond duty to unreserved obedience.

With No Claim on God

In looking at this passage we see very clearly that we have no claim on God. God is not put in our debt. We have a duty to God. But we must go beyond that duty in love.

Obedience has its own reward; but we cannot be obedient for the thought of reward. We do not establish claims on God by being obedient to him or in doing our duty to him.

Many people have a "balance sheet" kind of religion and morality. Goodness and Christian service are conceived in terms of credits and debits on a balance sheet. With this kind of mentality, after a person has done a certain amount of good, he thinks that God is in his debt. The Jewish people of the first century had a concept of this nature. But it has not died out with the first-century Jews. Many people today still feel that God is obligated to them because of what they have done for God. Goodness and obedience have their own reward. God does not owe us anything because of the service we have rendered to him.

One of the most bitter men I have ever seen was a Baptist deacon. He served as a deacon and a Sunday School teacher in a church where I had served as pastor. Then I moved to another church. He was a trucker; and one day I ran into him in the town where I was then serving. So we had a cup of coffee together.

Over the coffee I asked about his family. With little formal education himself, he had a great desire for his children to have a good education. Of the four that had reached the age to graduate from high school at that time, only one had graduated. Two of the children had married. One of those was already divorced and the other was married to a divorced person. Another daughter was unmarried, but had given birth to an illegitimate child shortly before. And she had kept the child.

After he related these things to me, with an increasing tone of disappointment, he then said, "Preacher, I just don't understand it. Ever since I have been a Christian I have tried to serve God. I have tithed my money. I have taught Sunday School. I have been a deacon. I have been faithful to the church. Why did God let these things happen to me?"

Obviously he felt that God owed him a better lot in life because of the service that he had given to God through the church. He could not understand why his children had turned out the way they did. It was as though he had tried to buy God's grace. It was as though he had tried to ensure good results for his family by the service that he gave to God in the church. He wanted to lay a claim on God.

But we live as Christian disciples with no claim on God. Because we follow him and conscientiously try to serve him we cannot claim from his exemption from the common lot of life.

Because the servant had faithfully cared for the sheep and plowed the field and then served the meal, he had no claim on the master. That was what he was supposed to do as a servant.

When we have attended church, tithed our income, served on church committees, sang in the choir, and taught in the Sunday School we have no claim on God. God does not owe us any special favor or any exemption from disaster, illness, or financial reverses.

I think of what I have called elsewhere "My Father's Stewardship

Testimony.'' [2] My father died in 1965, at the age of sixty-two. For many years he had been a Baptist deacon, as had his father before him. He took his Christian faith very seriously. Stewardship was an important part of Christianity to him. And to him stewardship meant tithing. No matter what else waited, he made sure that the Lord received his tithe.

While I never heard him put it into these words I think that he would have said that he tithed for three reasons: the Bible taught it; it was God's will; and it was right.

Tithing and church work did not ensure my father of a long life. Even though his father lived to within one week of ninety-eight years of age, he died at sixty-two. And that is not old.

Tithing did not make my father wealthy. At his death he did not leave a great deal of wealth, a lot of insurance, or vast land holdings. We always had food, clothing, and shelter, but our family was far from wealthy. Dad worked long, hard hours all of his life.

Tithing did not keep bad things from happening to him either. We had our share of crises, things breaking down, and such. My father died with cancer after eighteen months of suffering and several rounds of surgery.

If tithing did not make my father wealthy, ensure him of a long life, or keep him from suffering, why did he tithe? He tithed because he thought it was what he should do as a Christian. Since the Bible taught it, it was God's will, and it was right Dad faithfully tithed. But he did not try to make any special claim upon God.

The principle is the same for whatever aspect of Christian service you want to apply it. When we follow Jesus as disciples, we cannot make a claim upon God. We have to follow him for the sake of following him, not for the claims we can make because of it.

Rather than God being in our debt, we are always in God's debt. Paul reminded us of that when he said, "Or do you presume upon the riches of his [God's] kindness and forebearance and patience? Do you not know that God's kindness is meant to lead you to repentance?" (Rom. 2:4, RSV).

The kindness and patience of God with us even when we are at our best should lead us to repentance. We realize that all of life is lived in the sunshine of God's love and care.

A famous Scottish family has the motto "Saved to Serve." Duty is important. Many things are done out of a sense of duty that would never be done were it not for that sense of duty. Serving out of a sense of duty is not to be totally disparaged. But, as Christian disciples, we are aware that we must go beyond duty. We are indeed saved to serve. Because we are saved, we serve. Because we are disciples, we follow. When we consider the whole matter of discipleship and duty, we are aware that in following Jesus we must go beyond duty to unreserved obedience to God with no claim on God. That is discipleship.

9

What About Secret Discipleship?

"All the world loves a lover," is what the old proverb states. One thing is certain about a lover: it is never a secret. If one person loves another person, he will make it known in one way or another. Love does not keep secrets very well.

And that is one thing that has always made Joseph of Arimathea hard for us to understand from the Gospel accounts. We usually say that Christian discipleship is based on love and response to Jesus. But here is one who openly makes any claim to discipleship only after the death of Jesus. He is sometimes characterized as a "secret disciple." His claim to fame is that he provided the tomb in which Jesus was buried.

Joseph has been a figure of interest for some time. From whence did he come? What happened to him after he lent his newly made tomb to Jesus?

William Barclay in the second volume on the Gospel of Matthew in his familiar *Daily Study Bible* has passed on two interesting legends from England about Joseph.

According to one of these legends Joseph was sent by Philip from Gaul in A. D. 61 to preach the gospel in England. He is said to have come bearing with him the chalice which was used at the Last Supper. At that time it was supposed to have held the blood of Jesus which was shed upon the cross. That chalice was to become famous in the stories of the knights of King Arthur.

It was said that when Joseph and his band of missionaries had climbed Weary-all Hill and had come to the other side of it, they came to Glastonbury. There Joseph stuck his staff into the earth and from it grew the Glastonbury Thorn.

It is true that for many years Glastonbury was considered the holiest place in England. Pilgrimages are even now made there. The original thorn was hacked down by a Puritan, so the story goes, but the thorn that grows there now came from a shoot from it. Even today slips from this thorn are sent around the world.

According to the other story Joseph was a tin merchant. He came to the tin mines of Cornwall on frequent visits. The town of Marazion in Cornwall is sometimes called Market Jew. It is said to have been the center of a colony of Jews who traded in tin.

Also according to the legend, Joseph of Arimathea was the uncle of Mary, the mother of Jesus. Supposedly he brought the young boy Jesus with him on one of his voyages to Cornwall. William Blake thought of that when he questioned in his poem "Milton" if the feet of Jesus had in ancient time walked upon England's green mountains and if the holy Lamb of God had seen England's pleasant pastures and if Jerusalem were built there among the "dark Satanic mills" of the Cornwall tin mines.

These are legends, of course. But in addition to holding up the English hope that perhaps Jesus had been to England, they express something of the interest this elusive character, Joseph of Arimathea, brings.

Jesus died at about three o'clock on Friday afternoon. The Scriptures tell us that Joseph went in to Pilate and requested the body of Jesus. (Harking back to the Cornwall tin mine legend, if Joseph were the uncle of Mary he might have exercised the relative's right to claim the body of Jesus.) Pilate was amazed that he had died so quickly, but granted his request.

It was usually the custom to not even bury criminals. And Jesus was classed as a criminal at the crucifixion. They would often expose the bodies to the elements or they would be torn by vultures and wild animals. Some have even suggested that Calvary was called "The Place of the Skull" because of the presence of skulls laying around all over the place from former executions.

We are then told that Jesus was placed in Joseph's tomb which was hewn out of a rock and located in a garden. It had never been used before and was probably intended as a family burial place. Nicodemus and Joseph supplied one hundred pounds of spices for the body.

In the end Joseph declared himself for Jesus. Could he have been a secret disciple all along?

Is it possible to be a secret disciple? If discipleship is following Jesus, can one follow Jesus without making it known? Can you follow him and pattern your life after him in secret?

The Shame of Silence

Secret discipleship shows the shame of silence. Silence is often described as golden. There are times when silence is yellow. Silence can denote shame.

Joseph is called an "honourable counsellor" (Mark 15:43), or probably more accurately "a respected member of the council" (Mark 15:43, RSV). This is usually interpreted to mean that he was a member of the Sanhedrin.

We do know that he was rich. He was able to afford his own tomb. And he had to be influential, since he was able to get the body of Jesus from Pilate.

But as far as we know Joseph of Arimathea never spoke a word for Jesus during his life. Even though he was a wealthy, influential member of the Sanhedrin he never publicly spoke a word in Jesus' behalf during the whole affair. That is truly the shame of silence.

The shame of silence shows up in words of encouragement. How often we could encourage another person, but we fail to do so. Think of the encouragement that Joseph of Arimathea could have given Jesus had Jesus only known that he was with him. Perhaps he would not have publicly argued for Jesus, but if he had simply privately stated to Jesus that he had a friend on the council it would have encouraged him tremendously.

The book of Proverbs tells us that "A word fitly spoken is like apples of gold in pictures of silver" (Prov. 25:11). Many of those words "fitly spoken" should be words of encouragement.

Many a person works at a difficult task or carries a heavy load without any encouraging word from another. Whether written in a brief note or spoken in person or conveyed over the telephone, an encouraging word could lift a heart, lighten a load, and increase incentive.

I well remember one of my first evangelistic attempts in a rural church in central Louisiana. Having just graduated from college and soon to be enrolled in the seminary, I preached for a week there. During the week I stayed in the home of one of the faithful deacons of the church. While I preached about as well as I could, we did not have a single public decision during the week. At the conclusion of the final service, when the people came by to say nice things, this man came with tears in his eyes and spoke one word of encouragement that has carried me through many discouraging times, "Well done, thou good and faithful servant."

Thomas Carlyle was a man of brilliant intellect who made quite a scholarly contribution. But he was often ill-tempered and hard to please. After the death of his wife, he went home and read her diary. On page after page she recorded how he had been rough on her and how he had hurt her by his harsh words. As he turned the pages he is supposed to have said, "If only I had known. . . . If only I had known. . . ." From a positive standpoint we do know that encouraging words help people. It is a shame to keep silence when an encouraging word could be spoken.

Another obvious application of this principle has to do with Christian witnessing. It is a shame to keep silent when a word of positive Christian witness could have been given.

Joseph of Arimathea was obviously a man of some standing. His forthright witness to Jesus Christ could have carried a lot of weight with a lot of people. But he was silent. The witness he could have borne was lost. The people he could have influenced for Jesus were never reached. That is the shame of silence.

One of the refreshing things about President Jimmy Carter has been his forthright witness for Christ. In his book, *Why Not the Best?* he indicated that he had always joined the other deacons in the First Baptist Church of Plains, Georgia, in visiting the nonchurch families in their community prior to the annual revival.

One time he was invited to make a speech in a nearby church on the subject of "Christian Witnessing." As he worked on the message he thought he would add up the number of personal visits he had made for God. At that time he had been out of the Navy fourteen years. He had visited an average of two families a year. Assuming two parents and three children per family that would make a total of one hundred forty visits. Proud of that he wrote the figure in his notes.

Then he remembered the 1966 governor's campaign when he ran unsuccessfully for the governor of Georgia. Since it was late when he decided to enter the campaign he determined to try to overcome the handicap. Leaving everything he cared for, he and his wife went in opposite directions shaking hands and trying to meet as many Georgia voters as possible. Working sixteen to eighteen hours a day at the end of the almost-successful campaign they had met more than three hundred thousand Georgians.

The comparison struck him. In three months he had made three hundred thousand visits for himself and one hundred forty visits for Christ in fourteen years! Would you dare to make the same comparative figure? There is a shame to our silence in witnessing.

The Crisis of the Cross

Secret discipleship also shows us the crisis of the cross. It takes the cross to bring us to the personal crisis so that we see ourselves as we really are and are willing to make a change. For each one of us, the cross always brings a crisis. It always demands a decision. No one can stand before the cross and leave the same. It changes you in one way or another.

We are told in Mark 15:43 that Joseph "waited for the kingdom of God." This would mean that he was a religious man who was looking for God's salvation. He was waiting for God to reveal himself in some decisive way. He desperately wanted the kingdom of God to come on earth.

But it only came through the cross! This was probably the very last way that Joseph would have looked for the revelation and the power of God. This was the least likely spot for an understanding of the work and the way of God in the world. But the cross provided the crisis that made him realize that Jesus truly was something special.

Evidently Joseph was a witness of the crucifixion. This was the thing that changed him from an admirer of Jesus to a believer in Jesus.

It bears out the words of John 12:32, "And I, if I be lifted up from the earth, will draw all men unto me." Having seen Jesus lifted up on the cross, Joseph was drawn to him. He saw him as the Savior. The cross provided the crisis that brought decision to his life.

In *God's Gold Mines,* C. Roy Angell recorded a story told by Clifton J. Allen, who for many years was associated with the Sunday School Board of the Southern Baptist Convention. The story concerned Allen's father and uncle who were small boys when their parents moved out West. They had lived there for several years before the two boys were allowed to drive the wagon to the nearest town for supplies.

One time when they drove the wagon to town they did not get started quite early enough. On their way home a severe snowstorm overtook them just at dark. In a matter of minutes they were lost. Since they were not dressed warmly enough for a blizzard they faced the danger of freezing to death if they did not reach home in time. Their father went out to search for them, but he did not dare go out of the sight of the lights from home lest he get lost in the driving snowstorm. Their mother put a light in every window of the house.

She also prayed earnestly to God to save her boys.

Finally, one of the boys saw a faint light and used that as a guide to bring them to their own home. They were saved from the storm by a light in the window.

The next day their father cut down the tallest tree he could handle. After trimming off the limbs, he made a light pole out of it and set it in the front yard. On its top he put a pulley with a rope attached. Every night he lighted a lantern and pulled it to the top of the pole to act as a beacon to guide anyone who might be lost on the prairie.

Lost in our sins, confused in the direction for life, with all sorts of currents swirling around us we look for the light to guide us. It is found in Christ. By his death on the cross he assured us of God's love. By his death on the cross he ensured our eternal life through faith in him. Life takes on meaning when it is submitted to the one· who gave his life on the cross.

The cross forms the crisis for each one of us that demands that we examine life carefully. Then we can see, as did Joseph, that Jesus is one to be believed, followed, and served, not just admired as a good teacher or a fine man.

The Demand of Decision

The question of secret discipleship also brings to light the demand for decision. At some time, a decision has to be made about Jesus Christ. Not to decide is to decide. Our relationship with Jesus always demands a decision from us.

It is impossible to serve God in silence. Joseph did not apparently have a word to say for Jesus when he was alive. But he had a tomb for him in death. A decision was demanded if he were to serve Christ at all.

According to Mark 15:43 Joseph "went in boldly unto Pilate, and craved the body of Jesus." When the decision was demanded, he made it boldly.

Boldness in announcing a decision is one of our greatest needs. Some decisions cannot be reached with timidity and held in secrecy.

They simply have to be announced. An engagement is boldly announced. A marriage is boldly announced. The birth of a baby is boldly announced. And discipleship, for it to be discipleship, must be boldly announced also.

Some years ago Elton Trueblood told about a man who entered Earlham College as a freshman some years past the normal age for a freshman college student. He had come to the college from a rather well-paying job at a brewery. When someone asked him why he had entered college so late, he replied that he had made up his mind that he did not want to spend his life making beer. There was something more to life than that; if he were ever going to do more, a decision was demanded.

The boldness of this decision brings a compulsion to serve Christ. After his death the only way Joseph knew to serve Christ was to provide him with a burial place. During our lives there are many ways that we can carry out this compulsion to serve Christ.

Baptists are rightfully proud of our contribution to religious liberty in the United States. This came neither easily nor cheaply. The early Baptists felt that they had to share what they had seen, heard, and experienced with Jesus Christ. There was no secret discipleship with them.

The colonial dissenting preachers in Virginia were required to get a license from the authorities to preach. Many Baptists refused to do this, saying that they had been licensed by King Jesus which made any license by King George unnecessary. And many of them suffered persecution because of it.

One of the most notable cases was that of James Ireland in Culpeper County, Virginia, in 1796. Soon after coming to Culpeper County he was warned to quit preaching. But after counting the cost of freedom or confinement, liberty or a prison, he determined to suffer for Christ if necessary since he had ventured all for him.

Having been seized when he preached, the judge decided to make an example of him. Despite his weakness from cold and improper food he preached through the bars of the small iron gate in the jail.

They hacked his outstretched hands with swords as he preached. They whipped others outside the jail so that he could see and hear their distress as a warning of the future punishment he might receive. They uncovered a plot to blow up the jail. A physician rescued him from attempted poisoning. His tormentors burned pods of Indian pepper to smoke him to death. Yet he continued his witness and wrote letters to his friends headed, "From my palace in Culpeper." At length he was released. But he was too weak from the experiences to resume preaching with his old power.

When decision is demanded, it must be made with boldness. Then it can be carried out with the power of God.

Secret discipleship? No way. When one is a disciple of the Lord Jesus Christ, it must show. There is no way that it can be successfully hidden.

The question has been asked many times before, particularly to youth groups, "If you were accused of being a Christian would there be enough evidence to convict you?" If there would not be enough evidence to convict you, then your commitment and your discipleship could surely bear examining.

Joseph of Arimathea could not remain a secret disciple. He had to declare for Jesus Christ. If you are a disciple of Jesus, you can not be one in secret either. Make your declaration boldly.

10

The Defection of a Disciple

Country and western music is filled with the sad songs of someone who loved and left. There is something that hurts and saddens when one who had vowed allegiance and love instead departs, forsaking the one to whom he had pledged his life.

If there is sadness when a lover leaves or a father forsakes, how much sadder it is when a disciple defects. The very nature of discipleship indicates that one would follow Jesus to the very end. The end, however, for some has been short.

Of all the Lord's creation man should have the best view of time. It is man who should be able to measure his life span against the impact of eternity. For man is the only of God's creatures who is able to reason, to remember, and to apply with logical reasoning the things that he has remembered. To man alone lies the responsibility of some grasp of infinitude. He alone can measure his life, not by what happens now, but by eternity.

But even with this mark of superiority over the animals, we have been slow to use it. Too often we look at our lives only in the present situation, not against the backdrop of eternity. Too often we fail to think of the ultimate outcome of an action but only of its present implications.

Living for the present we never build for the future. We get our food in disposable containers; we use throwaway ball-point pens to write and disposable razors to shave; we diaper our babies in dispos-

able diapers; we design our consumer products with built-in obsoles-
cence; and we go to school in temporary buildings.

The Europeans have criticized us for building only for the present.
They say that the buildings we construct in our cities are not designed
for the centuries. And they are right.

But the same can be said for our lives. We live for the present.

I think that is the import of the one rather haunting verse in the
closing words of Paul's second letter to Timothy. He wrote, "For
Demas hath forsaken me, having loved this present world" (2 Tim.
4:10).

This verse has always bothered me. Paul asked his young preacher
friend to come to him quickly. The scene is most probably a prison in
Rome. This is a probable second imprisonment for Paul. This time
there is not a private house as there was in the first imprisonment. In
all probability it is a dark, damp, and cold prison cell. He asked for
his coat and his books. He told about all those who had left him while
he was imprisoned. He was left alone with only his physician, Luke.
And the old, persecuted preacher called for his young son in the
ministry.

But did you notice? Of all those whom he mentioned who had left,
about five or six, only for one person has he a word of implied
condemnation—Demas.

Demas is mentioned only three times in the Scriptures. In the book
of Philemon he is mentioned as a fellow laborer. In Colossians Paul
related that Luke and Demas joined in his greeting to the Christians
at Colosse. Then here in 2 Timothy there is an air of sadness when
Paul wrote, "Demas hath forsaken me."

We are not given the specific reason for Demas' departure. Some
say it was because of a lack of courage; others say it was because of a
love of money and gain. Some feel he may have alleged a call from
Thessalonica; others think that he just preferred the comfort and
security away from Rome to the hardships and danger at Rome with
Paul.

There is some speculation also about how far Demas left. There is an ancient legend that says that he became a pagan priest in Thessalonica. Some have said that he renounced the Christian faith entirely. In the minds of many he did not leave Christianity, he just left Paul to return to his home in Thessalonica.

I have always wondered why he left, whether he just left Paul or forsook the faith, and now I think I have found the key in the phrase, "Having loved the present world." Like so many of us, Demas was living for the present. To live for the present you do not have to renounce your Christian faith. You can just prefer the comfort and security of an action that benefits you for the moment and leave a place of responsibility or leave a task undone.

Unfortunately, there are times when we witness the defection of a disciple. Having a son who is a distance runner, I have spent a good bit of time watching people run long distances. In many races there are people who start off well but never make it to the finish line. My own high school track coach told us that any runner who did not finish the race would have his plate broken that night. He would not eat with the team. That is pretty strong motivation for teenaged boys.

Whenever there is a defection of a disciple, whether for a time or an apparent renunciation of the Christian commitment, a key to it is often that the individual is living for the present. He is able to see only the moment and not the long view. Even Jesus told in the parable of the soils about some seeds that would quickly spring up, only to wither and die because of lack of depth.

Living for the present, some defect from discipleship. Why?

Seeking the Thrill in Life

One of the ways in which people defect from discipleship by living for the present is in seeking the thrill in life. All of life is lived for the thrill of the moment.

Our generation is pleasure mad. The pursuit of pleasure results in the spending of millions of dollars and the expending of great amounts of energy and time. Anything that gives pleasure can immediately attract a following. As Foy Valentine of the Southern

Baptist Convention Christian Life Commission has said, people are looking for new nerve endings to excite.

In this pursuit for pleasure those things that are lasting are overlooked. The music, for instance, of this day will not stand the test of time. It is definitely not the music for the centuries. An authority on hymnology recently indicated that church hymn writing had fallen on bad times. The unmetered poetry and modern syncopation in music were the culprits, according to this authority. Seeking a momentary thrill, the lasting is forsaken.

A few years ago a twenty-seven-year-old man was convicted of three brutal robbery-slayings in Islip, New York. He indicated that he got a thrill out of killing. When asked how he spent the money, he said that he had spent one third on women, one third on liquor, and one third on foolish things. Seeking the thrill in life he had followed destructive measures.

It is a sad commentary on our society and on our discipleship to say that the most important thing is that which produces a momentary thrill.

Some years ago Elton Trueblood observed that we can discover what people do not have by what they frantically seek. He cited the popularity of Rabbi Liebman's *Peace of Mind* and Norman Vincent Peale's *A Guide to Confident Living* as illustrations. He also suggested in his *Signs of Hope in a Century of Despair* that the modern frame of mind is revealed by what draws the crowds. At one major university a high school basketball tournament outdrew Albert Schweitzer. And Alfred Kinsey, famed for his studies of human sexuality, was the only speaker who could outdraw a basketball game.

The result of seeking the thrill in life is a frustrating hopelessness. That is the reason there is no more joy in spite of all the attempts at pleasure.

No brief has to be made for the fact that people feel trapped in a sense of futility. Reference is constantly made to "the rat race" of life. Alcoholism and drug addiction are ways of life for many people as they attempt to anesthetize themselves against life. Irresponsibility is rife. Absenteeism becomes a major problem in many industrial concerns.

There is a search for a center in life, for something about which ☞ life can be built. Seeking the thrill where there is no joy and satisfaction has caused many people to lose the very thing that can always bring them back to center—a vital, vibrant, viable faith in Jesus Christ.

Some missionaries are supposed to have landed on the beach of a South Sea island. When they landed on the beach, they began to collect driftwood for a fire. Then they built the fire and warmed themselves around it. Soon they noticed a group of chimpanzees who were dragging up branches and arranging them as though for a fire. Then they warmed their hands and their feet at the pile of wood. But there was no fire! So often we have gone through the motions but have lacked the fire of God's Holy Spirit in our actions. When one seeks only the thrill in life, this is what happens. There is no fire. There is no depth. Life takes on a certain hopelessness. And there is a defection from the one who can give meaning and direction to life.

Emphasizing the Trivial in Life

When one lives for the present, he has emphasized the trivial in life. We constantly do battle against the problem of the good overcoming the best. There are many things that might be good things in themselves. But God has called us to the best.

President Jimmy Carter told of his application for the Navy nuclear submarine program in his book *Why Not the Best?* In an interview with Admiral Hyman Rickover, Carter sat in a large room with Rickover for more than two hours. Rickover let him choose the subjects they would discuss. Very carefully he chose those things about which he knew the most at the time—current events, seamanship, music, literature, naval tactics, electronics, gunnery. Then Rickover began to ask him a series of questions of increasing difficulty. In each instance, he soon proved to Carter that he did not know as much about the subject as he thought he did. Always looking him right in the eye, he never smiled. Carter was soon saturated with sweat.

Finally he asked a question Carter thought could help him redeem himself. He asked how he stood in his class at the Naval Academy. He had done very well and swelled his chest with pride when he replied that he stood fifty-ninth in a class of eight hundred twenty. Instead of congratulations, Rickover asked him one more question. He asked if he had done his best.

Before answering that he had, Carter remembered those times when he could have learned more about the allies, the enemies, weapons, strategy, or whatever the subject. So he replied that he had not *always* done his best.

Rickover looked at him a long time, then turned his chair around to end the interview. He asked one final question, which Carter could neither answer nor forget. That question was, "Why not?"

And why have we not done our best for God? Perhaps it is because we have emphasized the trivial so much in life that we have obscured the best. Arguing about and concerned over the trivial, we have never really gotten around to following Jesus in obedient, decisive discipleship.

A president of Andover-Newton Theological Seminary once said that if the church suffered from any ailment it was that of triviality.

So much of church programming, activity budgeting, and the expenditure of energy is for that which is, in the end, trivial. How things are done seems many times to take precedence over what things are done in the name of Christ.

Convenience is put over consistency. Expediency becomes the word that governs life. Rather than searching our actions for consistency with the principles of Christ we do rather those things that are most convenient for us.

Early in my ministry I was faced with a particular church problem that worried and bothered me. I tried to figure out the right solution. But I kept being faced with the problem of possibly offending some of the church people with the decision. I sought out my college Bible teacher and laid out the problem before him. Of course, he did not tell me what to do. But he did give a principle in making that decision that helped then and has helped many times since then. He said, "You will have to decide whether you will follow what is expedient or your convictions."

Perhaps this was Demas' problem. Was he to be consistent with his commitment and convictions and stay with Paul or would he choose the convenient and return to Thessalonica? Apparently he choose the convenient.

And we cannot help but think of the modern missionary martyr Bill Wallace. When Bill Wallace served in China as a medical missionary under appointment by the Southern Baptist Convention Foreign Mission Board, he could have chosen the convenient. He could have left at many points. But he did not. When the Communists despaired of changing him and his witness for Christ, they decided to end it. After being imprisoned on false charges he finally died in prison. His Chinese friends said that his gravestone should say that he was like Jesus. It does bear a witness with these words, "For to me to live is Christ."

It comes down to where a person will place his love. The love of Christ must be more compelling than the love of the world that would draw us away from Christ. Whatever would crowd out Christ and draw us away from him would fit into the definition of the world. Christ is to be loved supremely.

There are commentators who think that 2 Timothy 4:10, in which it is stated that Demas forsook Paul because he loved the present world, was purposely contrasted with 2 Timothy 4:8, where reference is made to those who love Christ's appearing. Whether purposely made or not, the contrast is there. Some have loved the appearing of Christ and look for him. Others have loved the present world and defected from him. A proper love for Christ will ensure that one will not live for the present.

Forgetting the Eternal in Life

It must also be said that the defecting disciple who lives for the present is forgetting the eternal in life. Life is not lived on one dimension alone—the present. Life also has an eternal element to it that cannot be forgotten.

In forgetting the eternal you forget that present actions have future results. Scarcely any action has simply a present result. It also has results that carry over into the future. The tragedy of living for the present is that the future results do not seem to concern the individual.

One of the best biblical illustrations of this principle happened when King Hezekiah of Judah showed off his strength to the Babylonians. In the story recorded in Isaiah 39, Hezekiah showed all his treasure—the gold, the silver, the precious oil, and the armory—to a delegation of visiting Babylonians who came to see him after his recovery from a serious illness. Later Isaiah, the prophet, asked the king what he had showed them. The king replied that he had showed them all of his treasure. Then Isaiah revealed to him the foolishness of that action. He prophesied that all of that treasure would one day be carried to Babylon and that even his sons would be carried captive. To that Hezekiah replied with one of the most shortsighted statements in all of history, " 'The word of the Lord which you have spoken is good.' For he thought, 'There will be peace and security in my days' " (Isa. 39:8, RSV).

Actions truly have future results. It is good for parents to remember this with their children. And it is good for Christians to remember this in their actions.

But how can we endure as Christians? How can we hold out in the face of the allurement of the present world? Endurance is in the hands of God. It is never that we endure in our own strength because of the power of God in our lives.

The very nature of the conversion experience—that it is a new birth—indicates something of the secret of endurance. When one has been born into the family of God, he cannot be unborn.

That one in whose hands we have placed our lives is stronger than any other power. In Romans 8, Paul reminded us in unforgettable language that nothing can separate us from the love of God in Christ Jesus. Conjure up all of the strong and separating forces you can imagine. None of them is stronger than God. God is stronger than all. In his hands there is endurance.

Again the prophet Isaiah has a strengthening word: "But now thus says the Lord, he who created you, O Jacob, he who formed you, O Israel: 'Fear not, for I have redeemed you; I have called you by name, you are mine. When you pass through the waters I will be with you; and through the rivers, they shall not overwhelm you; when you walk through fire you shall not be burned, and the flame shall not consume you. For I am the Lord your God, the Holy One of Israel, your Savior'' (Isa. 43:1-3, RSV).

Or as someone has expressed it poetically:

> Let me no more my comfort draw
> From my frail grip on Thee;
> In this alone rejoice with awe,
> Thy mighty grip on me.

In forgetting the eternal we also forget that destiny is determined by decision. The eternal destiny of the individual is determined by the decision that he makes to accept or to reject Jesus Christ as personal Savior. All of life's destiny is determined by the decisions that are made one by one.

Likely Demas did not just get up one morning and announce that he loved the present world more than the service of the Savior, and defect. That decision was probably made slowly over a period of time. One small decision added to another, added up to the decision that he would defect from his discipleship.

But there is one more very significant thing that must be remembered about Demas and any other defecting disciple. Even though apparently they have left active discipleship, the door is always open. He could always have come back. Christ will receive anyone who repents and returns.

Any defection can be a temporary defection. Any departure from Christian service can be a temporary departure. God has the ability and the willingness to forgive and accept when anyone returns to him.

Any number of people have turned to God as did the prodigal son to say, "I want to come home. I want to come back." And God has answered in the affirmative to each one of them. Any one of us can come back. That is the wonder and the glory of God's grace. In this case, you can go home again. You can go home to God's grace.

I read of a father who had suffered deep grief because his son had left home in a rebellious attitude to join a group of young people in a commune. Although the father had asked the authorities to help him in locating his son the search was unsuccessful. It was determined, though, that the son had moved to a certain major city.

The father went to the city and made a list of all the places frequented by young people who shared the life-style of his son. Following this, the father took his own portrait to a studio and had many prints made. He wrote across each picture: "All is forgiven. I love you. Come home. Dad."

Then he went to each of the bars and the dives on his list and added his picture to those hanging on the walls, after asking permission to do so.

The son came into a bar and was stunned to see his father's picture and message. It touched his heart. He felt a flood of sorrow sweep over him for the suffering he had caused his father. He realized that his rebellion was resulting in wasting his life and leading him into a life of bleak oblivion. The son counted his money, pawned his possessions, and bought a bus ticket that would take him home. You can go home again if you are going home to God.

George Beverly Shea in his autobiography, *Then Sings My Soul*, indicated that his preacher father had a notebook on his lap when he died. It was opened to these words that he had written in it: "Life has been wonderful. The promises of God precious. The eternal hope glorious.'' How much of a contrast that is with the sadly haunting words describing Demas.

For any disciple who contemplates defecting from his discipleship there is the reminder that life cannot be lived for the present. Life is lived *in* the present. The present has meaning both to God and to the individual. But life cannot be lived exclusively *for* the present. It has an eternal dimension to it that cannot be overlooked.

For life to be lived at its best in the present and for eternity it must be lived with Christ at the center.

11

The Worth of Discipleship

In 1974, famed motorcycle stuntman Evel Knievel attracted a great deal of attention by an attempt to jump over Snake River Canyon in Arizona on a motorcycle. For days newspapers carried accounts of the publicity buildup and the personal preparation for the jump. When the time for the jump came, it was televised. Riding a specially-designed and specially-made jet motorcycle, Evel Knievel attempted to jump across the canyon. He did not make it.

He was not the only one who was unsuccessful in his attempt to hurdle obstacles, however. A few days after the jump an Associated Press release in the newspapers pictured a number of children with bodily injuries. The one thing in common with the children and their injuries was that each one had obtained the injury by imitating Evel Knievel by attempting to jump over obstacles or ditches on their bicycles.

To Evel Knievel the attempted jump across the canyon was worth his life. To the children who imitated him, the jump across their particular obstacle was worth their lives. It was a risk. But for them the risk was worth it. It was worth their lives.

Is this what you would want to give your life for? Is it really worth your life to give it for something that is spectacular and attention-getting, to say the least, but also fleeting and temporary? If it is going to cost your life, why not give your life for something that is more worthwhile? For a start, give your life in Christian discipleship in following Jesus.

Is discipleship worth your life? It is. In fact, that is exactly what discipleship will cost you—your life. The worth of Christian discipleship is seen in its cost. It will cost your life in commitment and obedience to Jesus Christ.

Jesus made this quite clear in three related interviews in Luke 9:57-62. Earlier in the same chapter (vv. 23-24) Jesus had laid down the requirement for discipleship.

The basic requirement of discipleship is that you give your life to Christ. It is that you must be willing to give up your life for him. When Jesus said that one must pick up his cross daily to follow him, he made a reference to death. The cross might be an item of decoration for us. For Jesus, as for others who lived under Roman rule in the first century, the cross was an instrument of death.

We were renovating the worship center of our church when the representative from the stained-glass company came by. As we discussed the design for the stained-glass window that would go above the baptistry she asked if we could not work in a subtle cross on either side of the baptistry. A subtle cross? How do you have a subtle cross? There is no way that you can die subtly, especially on a cross. Death on a cross was a wrenching, wretched way to die. The Romans had crucified enough people in Palestine for all of those who heard Jesus to know exactly what he meant when he said that anyone who followed him would have to take up his cross. It meant that he had to be willing to die. In public executions the person to be crucified carried his own cross to the place of execution as Jesus did to Calvary. Those who heard him knew what he meant.

To follow Jesus is to say no to yourself. It is to identify with him in his death by your death to self. It is to exercise a passionate loyalty that would even cost your life.

After enunciating this principle, Jesus gave concrete examples of it. From the interviews with these three men we have some specific instances of the meaning of the demand for self-denial and self-surrender to the Savior. I had an English teacher in college who would not be thrown off the trail with vague generalities. When asking a question, she would also ask for concrete examples to be presented.

Not one of the three men mentioned in this passage were willing to give the passionate loyalty to the kingdom of God that it required. While willing to follow along behind Jesus they were not willing to follow him. But discipleship is following Jesus. It will involve some risk. It is worth your life. And it will cost you your life.

Count the Cost

The first man was a volunteer. He came up to Jesus and volunteered to follow him. To him Jesus said, "Count the cost."

He likely thought that by following Jesus the road would lead to power, success, and glory. Instead it led to Gethsemane and Golgotha. Jesus cautioned him to know what was involved in following him, to count the cost.

Jesus was very popular at this time. Any number of people followed in the crowds listening to his teaching, marveling at his miracles, and approving of his ability to get ahead of the religious authorities. But the time had come to separate the serious from the curious. There had to be a division between those who really meant business and the hangers-on.

The cost of discipleship is your life. You give up your life and your selfish, self-serving claims to follow him. It means such a total commitment of self to him that it was as though you had given up life itself for him.

This means that you will have to change some dreams. All of us dream dreams. But if you are to follow Christ the dreams must be changed from self-centered dreams to Christ-centered ones. We are to dream dreams for Christ. They are the dreams of what Christ can do in a life and what Christ can do in the world through the witness and the ministry of his people.

A sage once gave some advice to a young man. "What you need is a dream in your eyes," he said. "Will it hurt?" the young man asked. "No more than most dreams do!" replied the wise old man.

In counting the cost and following Christ, the demand is to go all out for him. In the terms of Jesus' day that was the willingness to assume a cross. In the terms that our day can understand it means to give him all that we have, to put out 100 percent for the Savior.

My football career was anything but long and distinguished. It was, in fact, limited to two seasons in the City Recreation Department leagues. The first season I played in the 105-pound league which meant that no one on the team could weigh more than 105 pounds. The next season I moved up to the 125-pound league which had a weight limitation of 125 pounds. I could have played in that league the next year too, but I was too old. I did not outgrow the league; I just outlived it.

We had a fine football team that year in the 125-pound league. We won the city championship. And we had a quarterback who distinguished himself by not getting tackled the whole year!

Our coach was a young man who was then still a college student, majoring in physical education. He was also in the Marine Reserves. As I recall, that was in 1950, the year the Korean conflict broke out.

We had made it to the midpoint of the season without a defeat. Then we were to play the next toughest team in the league before we started repeating teams. Also, in that week, the coach received notice from the Marine Reserves that he was called to active duty.

On the night of that game he gathered his team around him. Then he made a speech that would have been a credit to Knute Rockne. He said, "Boys, you know that I have been called to active duty in the Marine Corps. That means that I will be sent to Korea. You know what is happening in Korea. That means that I may not come back. And that means that this is the last game that I will coach you. It might be the last football game I will ever coach. So get in there and win this one for coach!" There never has been a more motivated bunch of 125-pound bruisers. We could have beat Louisiana State University that night! And we won it for coach.

As we follow Jesus he calls us to give our best. It is not something that one does unadvisedly. He is cautioned to count the cost. Counting the cost, when following Jesus in discipleship the very best, your all, is demanded.

Determine the Priority

The second man put family obligations before the kingdom of God. He wanted to bury his father before he followed Jesus. To which Jesus replied that the dead could bury the dead; he was to preach the kingdom of God. It would seem at first that Jesus was somewhat harsh in his response to the man. However, there is every possibility that his father was in good health and looking forward to a long life. He was stating that he would rather stay with his father as long as he lived. Then that family obligation would be completed and he would be free to follow Jesus.

William Barclay told of an English officer in the Middle East during the days of British dominance there who discovered a brilliant Arab young man. He was so brilliant that he could have attended Oxford or Cambridge University on a scholarship. In fact, such a scholarship was offered to him. He answered that he would accept the scholarship after he had buried his father. At that time his father was in good health and no more than forty years of age.

But the point of Jesus' remark was that some decisions have to be made at the time offered. There is a moment of decision that has to be seized or forever missed. You have to determine the priorities in life.

The Bible seems to indicate, and our experience has borne it out, that there are two kinds of death. Physical death is one kind of death. We all die physically at some time. But spiritual death is also a possibility. Some people still live and function who are dead spiritually. Their priorities in life are such that spiritual matters and spiritual concerns never reach them. This prospective disciple was more concerned with the physical death of his father, at whatever time that might occur, than he was of his own spiritual death, due to the rejection of Jesus Christ.

Real discipleship depends on determining the priorities in life. While many things are good, helpful, and contributory to both life and society, they may not be the matters of primary priority.

Christian commitment is a matter of first priority for the disciple. Robert McCracken told the story of a Cavalier soldier in the service of King Charles of England during the English civil war. He had sold most of his property and had given a great deal of money to the Royalist cause. Then he was killed in battle with the Roundheads. His friends paid tribute to his memory with this epitaph which is found in an old churchyard in England, "He served King Charles with a constant, dangerous, and expensive loyalty." It may be expensive and dangerous to follow Jesus in total commitment. But that is a first priority for disciples.

The playwright Channing Pollock was walking along the street one day when he met an old friend. They had known each other as boys, but had been separated for many years.

As the two old friends talked the world-famed playwright saw this man, who was virtually unknown outside the circle of his intimate friends, in a new light. He talked with pride of his wife, his son, and his work. After they had finished their conversation Archie, the friend, walked away. Channing Pollock saw the sun shining on his blue serge suit and it looked for the world like he was dressed in shining armor.

Sometime later Channing Pollock wrote a play about his friend, Archie. It was called *Shining Armor*.

The action took place on two levels—a lower stage and an upper one. On the lower stage Archie struggled through the typical, tough processes of living and doing what he thought was right.

Toward the end of his life, and thus toward the end of the play, Archie's son got involved in a big shady real estate deal. Persons tried to interest him and, then in time, his father, Archie, in a shady transaction that would make them rich. The son argued that they could do it. They had been poor so long. They had suffered so much. Just that one time they could do it. But Archie said no. Then they argued. Archie had a heart attack and died on the spot. The son gathered his father up in his arms, wracked with tears.

Then the action shifted to the upper level and the viewer saw Archie clothed in shining armor contending against two evil knights. For a time it looked as though Archie would win, but then he weakened. Just as he was about to fall, his son leaped to his father's side and proceeded to fight off the evil knights, thus restoring Archie's confidence in the life he had tried to live before his boy.

That kind of commitment comes only when one has already determined his priorities. The Christian disciple acts on the principle of prior decision. He has already committed himself to Jesus Christ and to the principles of Christian discipleship. Those particular decisions do not have to be made each time they come up. They have already been made. The priority has already been determined.

Cut the Ties

The third potential disciple wanted to go back home and tell farewell to all of his family before he would follow Jesus. This man was not willing to cut the ties with the past. Tied closely to the past and to his culture he could not now move out into the future.

This is always a problem. It is more of a problem in a place that honors and reveres its past and among a people who are proud of their heritage. The past is important. It has shaped the present. The heritage is significant. We draw with strength and encouragement from the heritage that we share. But these can never be used to so tie us to the past that we can neither minister in the present nor plan for the future.

If we are to follow Jesus in the future, we discover that the future is now. Now is the time that we cut those ties that bind us to a culturally determined expression, or a religion that is shaped by society, to a faith that is willing to challenge its culture and a religion that will shape its society.

After the 1970 football season George Allen picked up his playbook and moved from Los Angeles to Washington, D.C. to become head football coach of the Washington Redskins. The Redskins had had only one winning season in the past fifteen years and had not been in the play-offs in twenty-five years.

Immediately he began to trade away Redskins and his draft choices (some of them twice) for a group of football players considered by others to be has-beens, washed-ups, and misfits. Allen figured that experience, not youth, would win football games. Other people figured he was out of his head.

Two years later George Allen and his tired old men had the last laugh. He welded the "Over the Hill Gang" into the champions of the National Football Conference and into the Super Bowl.

He used as his theme "The Future Is Now!"

This would not be a bad theme for possible Christian disciples to pick up as they consider the importance of following Jesus. It is not something to do when you have reached a certain age, or have reared the family and reduced your responsibilities, or when you have achieved certain goals. The future is now. Now is the time to cut the ties and to cast your lot with Christ.

There are times when Christ calls us to cut the ties with the past and all that binds us and sail out into the future. We make this trip with little luggage other than faith and with an eye toward the destination of following Jesus toward Christlikeness.

But in cutting those ties we follow Christ with hope. In *The Future of the Christian*, Elton Trueblood pointed out that many American settlers felt that they were led to America. It was necessary for them to cross stormy seas in uncomfortable sailing ships. They had much sickness and hardship. At times half of the passengers would die before the ship reached the New World.

After Robert Barclay was appointed nonresident governor by the proprietors of East Jersey colony he sent colonists from Scotland. Many of them, including his own youngest brother, died on the way. There is something appropriate about the fact that the ship which departed Aberdeen in August 1685, and on which David Barclay died, was called *America*. The American story, while it was a story of hardship and danger, was also one of hope.

True, there is a certain risk in following Jesus. But it is a risk that is not without hope. It is a risk that centers its hope in Jesus Christ.

A professional football quarterback was cut by his team. The coach called him in to tell him that they had seven quarterbacks. There were others who were bigger than he was, stronger than he was, faster than he was, and quicker than he was. Then he told the player that he could not use him.

As the player walked back to his quarters the other team members were coming out to practice. As he passed them, suited up for play, he kept thinking that the coach could not use him, but he could use them. Then he remembered that God was not like that. God never says to any one of us that he cannot use us.

But Jesus does let us know what is demanded when he does use us. It is worth your life to give your life in faith to Jesus Christ. Following Jesus makes life have full meaning. It gives significance to life. In following Jesus in discipleship, though, it is worth it. It is worth your life!

12

Discipleship for Decisive Days

Charles Dickens began *A Tale of Two Cities* with these words: "It was the best of times, it was the worst of times, it was the age of wisdom, it was the age of foolishness, it was the epoch of belief, it was the epoch of incredulity, it was the season of light, it was the season of darkness, it was the spring of hope, it was the winter of despair, we had everything before us, we had nothing before us, we were all going direct to Heaven, we were all going direct the other way." And he was not even talking about our time!

Surely no better description than this can be found for our days: "It was the best of times, it was the worst of times."

These are the best of times. Life expectancy is growing. Knowledge is exploding. Affluence is expanding. Leisure is increasing. Communications are tying us together.

But these are the worst of times. We are confused by the changes occurring faster than we can assimilate them. We are upset by the sociological engineering and the prospects of biological engineering. We are still bothered with the problems of poverty in an affluent society, exploding population in a crowded world, and ecological suicide. We are frightened by increasing crime rates, threats of revolution, government wrongdoing, and a developing society we do not always understand.

All observers, both religious and secular, feel that we are living in decisive days. It is not that we are unaware of this. We tried everything we knew to prepare us to enter the decade of the '70s. We analyzed, scrutinized, shaped, diagnosed, and prognosticated until we all felt that we had gone all the way through the decade before the first year was even completed. Without doubt, these are decisive days.

As Christians we are called to discipleship in decisive days. There are two things we cannot choose: we cannot choose the times in which we live, and as Christians we cannot choose whether we will be disciples. Discipleship is no option. When we accept Christ we assume discipleship. Since we live in these decisive days, we are called to a discipleship for decisive days.

The days in which the earliest disciples lived were decisive too. At a time when they were confused, frightened, and bewildered Jesus tried to prepare them for life in those decisive days without him. We call chapters 13-17 in John's Gospel "The Farewell Discourses." Notice particularly John 15:1-17.

One assurance that Jesus wanted the disciples to have was that even though he was not present with them physically they would not be thrown into the world alone. He would still be present with them spiritually. They would still have to depend upon him implicitly for life and strength.

It could well have been that Jesus and the disciples were walking across the Temple courtyard as they went from the upper room to Gethsemane when Jesus pointed to the Temple that had a golden vine above the entrance to the Holy Place and said, "I am the true vine . . . I am the vine, ye are the branches" (John 15:1,5).

The symbol of the vine was a familiar one to all Jews. Israel had been symbolized many times in the Old Testament as the vine of God. However, the prophets had never spoken of Israel as the vine apart from the idea of degeneracy.

So Jesus assured us that he was the true vine and that we have a relationship with God the Father only through him. The believer is united by faith to Jesus Christ and draws from him all his strength, all his sustenance, all his life. Like the intention of the relationship between Israel and God, the relationship between the believer and Christ was to be fruitful.

This is our directive for discipleship for decisive days: we must exist as Christians in a faith relationship with Jesus Christ that draws all our strength from Him. From this conversation of Jesus with his earliest disciples I think we can draw some guidance for us present disciples about discipleship for these decisive days, these days that are both the best of times and the worst of times—our times.

Commitment

Discipleship for decisive days demands that we know where our commitment is.

Jesus made it very clear: we must be committed to him. Our basic commitment as Christians is to Jesus Christ as Lord. The earliest Christian confession of faith was "Jesus is Lord." This must be our present confession of faith.

It is only as we abide in him that we are able to have life itself; it is only as we abide in him that we are able to function properly, to be fruitful; it is only as we abide in him that we are given sustenance and strength. The continual process of pruning, growing, and developing comes through our relationship with Christ. The lordship of Christ in our lives is essential.

Insistence on the lordship of Jesus Christ will ensure that we maintain our belief that Christian faith is basically a personal relationship with Christ as Savior. As Baptists we have insisted that people are not saved through churches or institutions, but through faith in Jesus Christ. We have also insisted that the lordship of Christ cannot be delegated. We do not have popes, bishops, superintendents, or councils because we believe that each church and each believer must be free to follow Jesus Christ as Lord.

We are in danger of an erosion of this basic commitment to the lordship of Jesus Christ. We are moving in these days to a creedalism that in effect denies the ability of each believer to draw his direction from Christ, as a branch draws its strength from the vine, and instead decrees what a person must think and how he interprets God's Word. Baptists have never understood confessions of faith to be creeds that must be believed, but rather expressions of belief. The introduction to the *Baptist Faith and Message* adopted by the Southern Baptist Convention in 1925 and revised in 1963 said "we do not regard them [confessions of faith] as complete statements of our faith, having any quality of finality or infallibility." [1] This is consistent with our historic understanding of confessions of faith. While we cannot be so lax as to say that one can believe anything or nothing, it is dangerous to prescribe exactly how one must believe. This is a denial of our understanding of the lordship of Jesus Christ.

Commitment to Christ as Lord will determine the motivation for service. We will not act out of duty, nor compulsion, nor even from altruism. Motivational researchers have shown us that many things can move people. As Christians we must depend upon one thing: the love of God and commitment to him. Anything else cheapens even Christian service to mere manipulation.

When Jesus Christ is Lord, our commitment to him is unconditional. Most of my father's working life was spent in a feed store. My father was a fine Christian. I will never be as good a Christian as my dad was. One time he was offered a job managing another feed store at a higher salary than he was then making. I asked him why he did not take it. He said, "Well, son, all these years I have been telling these people that Purina feed was the best for their livestock. If I started telling them something else now it would seem that I had been lying all this time." He had that kind of commitment to Christ, too. And that is the kind of commitment to Christ we must have.

If we are, indeed, branches from the vine drawing our life and strength from Christ we will have to be committed to Him as the Lord of all life. Jesus said it years ago, and we must remember it: "No man can serve two masters" (Matt. 6:24). And that is part of our problem: we have tried to divide allegiance. So in these decisive days we must know where our commitment is: it must be to Jesus Christ as Lord.

Community

Since we have a basic commitment to Jesus Christ, discipleship for decisive days demands that we know who our community is.

Christians are the people of God. Jesus said that he was the *true* vine. If Israel had brought degeneration, He would bring regeneration. In him all the promises are fulfilled. We do not exist as Christians in isolation. We are a part of a community of faith. Jesus indicated that all the branches exist in relationship with him. We are comrades in arms, brothers in Christ, fellow citizens of the Christian commonwealth, people in the community of faith.

While we come to faith in Christ individually and personally, we live and serve, witness and minister together. George Buttrick has said that if religion does not begin with the individual, it never begins; but if it ends with the individual—it ends. We are a community of faith in which we live out our Christian commitment in the world.

Since we are a community of faith, I think we will have to give more emphasis to the importance of the local church in these decisive days. Some of us have thought that the only expression of the church is local. We know that is a mistake. The community of faith is larger than my congregation. But the community of faith is expressed in a locality by a congregation. And, because of that, it is extremely important.

The whole Christian movement will stand or fall by what is done in churches located on the city squares, out in the suburbs, or on the forks of the branch. The local church provides the leadership, the finances, and the strength for everything that Baptists do. And we dare not forget that! We sometimes get so wrapped up in our projects and our programs that we forget that the institutions and the organizations exist for the churches and not that the churches exist for them.

Sometime ago Gerald Kennedy, bishop of the Los Angeles area of the United Methodist Church, appointed himself to a church. He said he wanted to close out his days in the active ministry not only as an administrator, but also as a pastor. Not long before he did that I had just gone through the agonizing process of trying to determine the direction of my ministry. And in one of the hardest decisions of my life I had declined an opportunity to perform my ministry in another area, in a way I had always thought I would like to follow, and felt compelled to remain in the pastorate. Even though I am not by nature a celebrity chaser, with that recent decision in the background I wrote Bishop Kennedy and expressed appreciation for what he had done and gratitude for the encouragement he had given those of us who try the difficult task of being a pastor. In his reply he said, "Thank you also for word about my going to a church. Not all of my brethren agreed with your opinion and I am so happy to have a word like yours just now. There is nothing like the local church and it will either be won or lost there as I am sure you will agree." In his book, *For Laymen and Other Martyrs,* Bishop Kennedy expressed this same thought. He said, "When you get down to cases, if anything is being done in a community it is being done through local churches and local congregations." [2]

Goodness knows, I am aware of all the things that are wrong with local churches. Some have said that the institutional church is sick. But it is not a sickness unto death; it can be a sickness unto renewal and new life. I know some thrilling stories of lives that have been changed, directions that have been established, witness that has been given, and ministries that have been performed. Some churches are doing some amazingly creative things in their attempt to be the people of God in this world. It is being done in the power of Christ. He reminded us that without him we could do nothing.

Of course the church, even the local church, especially the local church, has changed and will change. The church is a dynamic, living organism by nature, not a static organization. And change it must in this decisive decade. Significant discipleship will demand change. While it is true that churches have often resisted change, how tragic it would be if the one institution that does not change in the midst of all the other change is the church. We will have to give more attention to persons than programs, to the will of God and the direction of the Holy Spirit than to budgets and buildings. Change is the church's stock-in-trade. It is put here on the earth to change the world. But one thing must surely be constant: the lordship of Jesus Christ as the head of the church. We must be responsive to his leadership and dependent on his strength.

Since we are a community of faith, I think we will have to give more attention to our relationships together in these decisive days. Jesus gave us the commandment to love one another.

In these days we cannot forget that. We do not have the time or the personnel or the energy for the luxury of division. The pruning process is already going on. There are some things on which we do not all agree. That is all right. We never have. From the little I know about Baptist history I know that we have never all been agreed on the matters of pre-, post-, or a-millennialism, the relationship of evangelism and social action, alien immersion, open communion, or the historical-grammatical interpretation as opposed to an absolutely literal interpretation of the Scriptures. We do not have to be agreed on all the details. But we do have to be agreed on the necessity of salvation from our sins through Jesus Christ, the lordship of Jesus Christ, and our desire to serve him together. This is why we organized as a convention originally. And we must keep this purpose in mind. Colin Morris is probably right when he observed that your theology, plain or fancy, is what you are when the talking stops and the action starts.

We need one another. Those of us who have had more educational opportunities than others cannot be arrogant and snobbish. Neither can those of us who were not able to get much formal education be proud and defensive. The truth is that God can work without education and he can work with education. What he needs to work is someone willing to be used by him.

Have you ever noticed the number of times the apostle Paul used words that included a prefix signifying "togetherness"? Paul speaks of Christians as fellow heirs, fellow servants, fellow soldiers, fellow workers, and many other such expressions. R. E. O. White, the English Baptist writer, has listed thirty-four such designations.[3] We must work together if we are to work at all in this decisive time. The one thing that can bring people together in this divided and alienated world is the gospel of Christ lived in love.

What kind of people does God use? God uses all kinds of people. God can use the well-educated. Paul was certainly well-educated. And who can forget the contribution that men like John A. Broadus and E. Y. Mullins have made to Baptist life, both academic and practical? God can use the ill-educated. Think of John Bunyan, the tinker; William Carey, the shoemaker; and William Booth, the pawnbroker's assistant. They all lacked formal education, but each turned innumerable people to God. God can use the disfigured. George Whitefield was so cross-eyed that when he made the mistake of saying, "That man. That man I am looking at now," two men always came under conviction. God can use the obscure. Who knows the name of that preacher who urged Charles Haddon Spurgeon to "look and live"?

We exist as a community of faith, with the common experience of salvation in Jesus Christ and daily dependence on him. In these decisive days we must know who our community is for true discipleship.

Commission

Knowing who our community is, discipleship for decisive days demands that we know what our commission is.

Jesus told us that we are to be fruitful. In continuing the analogy that he used, we would see that our commission is to become like Christ in this world. The life is in the vine. When we draw upon the vine, rely upon him, we become like him. A Christian is not saved by bearing fruit, but one who is saved will bear fruit.

Our commission is to live in this world as a revelation of God through Jesus Christ, just as Christ came into the world as the revelation of God. In John's version of the Great Commission Jesus

said, "As my Father hath sent me, even so send I you" (John 20:21).
Jesus had a keen awareness that he was sent to do the will of God and
not his own; so we are sent to follow Christ's will and not our own.
Jesus was sent into the world to reveal God and to redeem men: we
are sent to reveal him and to be a redeeming influence among men
and to carry a redemptive message to men.

We live out our commission by showing love. Jesus gave a great
deal of importance to the life of love. William Barclay has remarked
that "Sometimes we live as if we were sent into the world to compete
with one another, or to dispute with one another, or even to quarrel
with one another. But the Christian is sent into the world to live in
such a way that he shows what is meant by loving his fellowman." [4]

In doing this we are not following an uncharted course, Jesus
showed us how to live in love. Never once did Jesus declare to
anyone: "I love you." But by his every action he showed love.
When he healed the sick, when he fed the hungry, when he gave
sight to the blind, when he blessed the children, when he stopped to
talk with the unknown and the unloved, when he died on the cross,
every action proclaimed in unmistakable terms: "I love you!" And
we must act in loving ways if we follow this Christ.

We can only live this kind of life by continual dependence on
Christ for life and strength. We are to bear the fruit of Christlikeness.
But the fruit bearing is conditioned on a vital relationship with Jesus
Christ. There is no way that we can know the joy of which he spoke,
the avenue of approach through prayer of which he spoke, and the
assurance of his love unless we maintain that relationship with him.

To do this we do not have to compete with one another or even to
count all of our results. We do have to determine that we will follow
his will in our lives, that we will be faithful to our own responsibility, and that we will seek to live in his strength.

I find help in a story passed on by C. Roy Angell in *God's Gold
Mines,* a story that shows the importance of faithfulness to our
commission.

Some years ago in Alabama at the state track meet interest was high for the mile run. It had been rumored that the state record might be broken. One of the teams had a boy who had come within a second of the record and was out to break it this time. As they gathered around the starting mark, all eyes were on that tall, good-looking young man with a gracious smile on his face. He was long of limb and with all the marks of an athlete of the first magnitude. However, at the far end of the starting line was a boy who was in every way a sharp contrast to this athlete. He was small of stature, his shoulders were bent a little, he was hollow-chested, and even his legs were not straight.

The command came, "On your mark, get set." Then the pistol cracked and the race was on. The fine athlete sprang into the lead at the very beginning, and with every lap he widened the distance between himself and the others. The little fellow steadily fell behind. When they came into the home stretch, the athlete sprinted the last hundred yards. As he broke the tape, a deafening roar went up from the crowd. He had broken the state record! Only a few others finished the mile; most of the runners had dropped out when they saw it was hopeless for them to win.

As the field crew were bringing out the hurdles to set up for the next race, suddenly one of the judges yelled, "Get those hurdles out of the way. This race is not over. Look!" Around the turn came that little boy, panting and staggering. Everybody in the audience stood silently and watched as he dragged up that last hundred yards and literally fell across the finish line. His face ground into the cinder track. One of the judges ran and turned him over on his back, took his handkerchief, and wiped the blood off his face. The judge asked him, "Son, why didn't you drop out back yonder? What are you doing in the mile race, anyway?"

Between gasps for breath, the boy answered, "My school had a good miler, but he got sick two or three days ago and couldn't run. The coach had promised to have a man in every event, so he asked me if I'd come and run the mile."

"Well, son," the judge continued, "Why didn't you just drop out, quit way back there? You were over a lap behind.''

He answered, "Judge, they didn't send me here to quit. They didn't send me here to win. They sent me here to run this mile, and I ran the mile.'' [5]

In these decisive days Christ has called us to be his disciples. He lets us know, as he assured those first disciples, that we are his disciples because he first chose us. He has chosen us to serve him and he has chosen us to serve him at this particular time in history.

Decisive days they are. Impossible days they are not. For discipleship in these decisive days we must have some things clear: where our commitment is, who our community is, and what our commission is. Our opportunity for discipleship is not to quit, not even to succeed, as the world might consider success, but to live for him—to live Christ's life in his power as he has sent us into the world in these decisive days.

Notes

Chapter 1

1. James S. Stewart, *King for Ever* (New York and Nashville: Abingdon Press, 1975), p. 124.
2. Courtney Anderson, *To the Golden Shore* (Grand Rapids: Zondervan Publishing Co., 1956), pp. 56-57.
3. C. Roy Angell, *God's Gold Mines* (Nashville: Broadman Press, 1962), pp. 11-12. Used by permission.

Chapter 2

1. While I cannot be sure about the source of this definition, it seems to me that it took shape during an address by J. P. Allen, now of the Southern Baptist Convention Radio and Television Commission before the Louisiana Baptist Convention some years ago. A story or two may also have come from that address.
2. Scripture quotations marked (RSV) are from the Revised Standard Version. © Division of Christian Education of the National Council of Churches of Christ in the United States of America, 1946, 1952. Used by permission.
3. Sam Shoemaker, *And Thy Neighbor* (Waco: Word Books, 1967), p. 147. Used by permission.
4. *Ibid.*, p. 149.

Chapter 3

1. Douglas MacArthur, *Reminiscences* (New York: McGraw-Hill Book Company, 1964), p. 18. © 1964, Time, Inc. All rights reserved.
2. Keith Miller, *The Taste of New Wine* (Waco: Word Books, 1965), pp. 38-39.
3. In William Barclay, *And He Had Compassion on Them* (Edinburgh: The Church of Scotland Youth Committee, 1955), p. 191.
4. Billy Graham, *Angels: God's Secret Agents* (Garden City, N.Y.: Doubleday and Company, 1975), p. 124.

Chapter 4

1. In James Dalton Morrison, ed. *Masterpieces of Religious Verse* New York: Harper and Row, 1948), p. 361.

Chapter 7

1. Phyllis McGinley, *"What Shall I Tell My Daughters?"* Reprinted by permission from the November 1959 issue of *Good Housekeeping.* © 1959 by the Hearst Company. Reprinted with permission from the November 1959 *Reader's Digest,* p. 162.
2. Quoted in Robert J. Hastings, *Hastings' Illustrations* (Nashville: Broadman Press, 1971), p. 100. Used by permission.

Chapter 8

1. Rudolf Bultmann, *Jesus and the Word* (New York: Charles Scribner's Sons, 1958), p. 79.

2. James E. Carter, *A Sourcebook for Stewardship Sermons* (Grand Rapids: Baker Book House, 1972), pp. 135-36. Used by permission.

Chapter 12

1. *Annual, Southern Baptist Convention,* 1963, p. 269.

2. Gerald Kennedy, *For Laymen and Other Martyrs* (New York: Harper & Row, 1969), p. 25.

3. R. E. O. White, *Apostle Extraordinary* (Grand Rapids: William B. Eerdmans Publishing Company, 1962), p. 107.

4. William Barclay, "The Gospel of John," *The Daily Study Bible* (Philadelphia: Westminster Press, 1955), II, 207.

5. C. Roy Angell, *God's Gold Mines,* (Nashville: Broadman Press, 1962), pp. 101-102. Used by permission.